To: Chri...

D0253625

The
Daily Motivator
To Go

I plan to read each
message one per day,
aloud to Maureen in
the morning during 2020.
   Each is short, but
great positive thoughts
add up.
   It's our hearts' desire to
bless you as we share a
special bond reading
together.
   We love you deeply!
            Richard & Maureen

The
Daily Motivator
To Go

by

Ralph S. Marston, Jr.

IMAGE EXPRESS INC.

Austin, Texas

The Daily Motivator To Go
By Ralph S. Marston, Jr.

Distributed by:
   Image Express, Inc.
   P.O. Box 66536
   Austin, TX 78766 USA
   Phone 512-401-4900
   Web: www.greatday.com/books

To read The Daily Motivator on the Internet, visit
www.DailyMotivator.com

ISBN 0-9664634-0-4
Printed in the United States of America

Contents

Get The Daily Motivator every day in your e-mail!

If you have access to the Internet, you can receive a fresh, new positive message in your e-mail, Monday through Saturday.

Success is not achieved in a one-shot attempt. The greatest accomplishments are the result of sustained, focused effort. *The Daily Motivator* e-mail edition helps to keep you focused on your own commitment to excellence. Each day, you receive a brief, positive message designed to make you stop and think about the possibilities for your own life.

Thousands of subscribers all over the planet depend on *The Daily Motivator* to get their day off to a positive start. And if you're on the 'net, you can, too!

For more information, visit *The Daily Motivator* website at

http://greatday.com

Introduction

The book you hold in your hands is a testament to the value of persistence and consistent effort. It was not written as a book, but rather as a series of daily messages, day after day after day. And not only was that the *method*, it is also a key *message* of this book. You can accomplish anything, *anything*, when you consistently apply effort for *as long as it takes*.

I have been publishing *The Daily Motivator* on the Internet, with six new messages every week, for more than two years. The daily motivational messages are now read each day by thousands of people all over the world. I'm constantly receiving phone calls and letters, asking for *The Daily Motivator* in book form. Now it is finally available! This book is a collection of more than 250 of my favorite articles from *The Daily Motivator*, printed and bound, and available now for the first time "off-line."

The individual messages are arranged by category into sections, making it easy for you to find the particular flavor of motivation that you're looking for at any given time. Adjacent messages reinforce each other, yet can be read and understood in any order.

Most authors attempt to write a book that readers will find impossible to put down. My purpose with this book is exactly the opposite. My goal is for you read a message, and then feel that you *must* put the book down and take action immediately to fulfill the possibilities in your life.

Whatever you want to have, whatever you want to do, whatever you want to become, you must take action today. The purpose of this book is to help you do that, by reminding you of the compelling possibilities that are present in every moment.

Have a great day, and enjoy the challenge of living life with passion, meaning and fulfillment.

Ralph Marston

Living day by day

What will today bring?

Today is full of opportunity. Everywhere you go, everything you do, every person you meet gives you the potential to make a difference — in your life, in the lives of others, in your community and in the world at large.

Welcome the challenges. Look for opportunities, in every situation, to learn and to grow. Delight in the beauty that is around you. Offer your sincere kindness and caring to others. This is the stuff of life.

You are fully alive and capable of making this day into whatever you want it to be. Though you often cannot control the situations that come along, you always can control the way you deal with them.

Every moment is your opportunity to express the wonderful, unique person that you are. Life is not in the fondly-remembered past. It is not in the hoped-for future. It is here and now. What you are now, is what you are.

Anything that may have previously held you back is now behind you. Today is your golden opportunity to fashion your life into what you want it to be.

Take a deep breath, put a smile on your face, and make it a great day.

Your future begins now

Today is a turning point in your life. The things you accomplish, the people you meet, the direction you set today, will have consequences far into the future.

One little bit of extra effort, made today, might change the rest of your life for the better. It would be a shame to miss the opportunity. So do all you can do today, and just a little bit more. Make that extra phone call. Look at that one additional report. Investigate that one additional possibility. Think of the difference it could make.

Each day affects all the ones that come after it. In your actions, in your thoughts, in your decisions, proceed as if today is the most critical day of your life. Because it is.

Relax

Have you ever noticed that when you don't need any new business, that's when you get it? And when you're desperately trying to increase sales, you can't seem to find any new customers? Sometimes it seems that the harder you try, the less effective you are.

It's possible to try too hard. To get so uptight and centered on something that you lose your effectiveness. Too much of anything will cause tunnel vision and burn-out. A healthy dose of perspective can be the cure.

Have you ever been "stuck", trying to figure out the answer to a tough problem? You work and work on it, and can't seem to find the answer. Then you take the weekend off, come back to it on Monday, and suddenly the answer is obvious. What happened? You got so close to the problem, you could not find the solution. And when you backed away for a little while, you were able to see much more clearly.

Of course persistence is vitally important in any enterprise, and so is balance. Don't get so obsessed with a particular outcome or detail that you lose balance. Learn to put all things in perspective. Sure you want to land that prospective customer, but not at the expense of your family and your health.

The trick is to remain focused on the outcome you desire, without becoming consumed by it. Learn to integrate all aspects of your life. Take time for fun, family and friends no matter how busy you are. And make it a point to learn something new each day in a field that's totally unrelated to what you're working on.

Learn to integrate a healthy balance into your life at all

The Daily Motivator To Go

times, especially the most stressful periods. You'll find that you can often get more done by trying a little less.

First things first

Here are a few suggestions to get you started on a productive, fulfilling day.

- Do the least desirable things first. You probably have a list of things to do today. Some of these things you're looking forward to doing. Some of them you frankly don't want to do. The first things you need to do are the things that you want to do the least. The tendency is to "put off" the disagreeable things until the very last minute. Doing them first, however, has lots of advantages. You'll probably get through them quicker, by doing them when you are fresh and haven't had time to get bogged down in a lot of other things. You'll get them over with, and won't waste time worrying about them all day. You'll be developing an important habit of self-discipline, of going right ahead and doing what needs to be done, no matter how unpleasant it is. And when you do get around to the work that you really want to do, you'll be able to put all your concentration into it, knowing smugly that all the unpleasant "have to do's" for the day are behind you.

- Confront your fears. Do something today that you've been afraid to do. Is there someone you're afraid to call? Is there some new skill you're afraid to try and tackle? Are you afraid to balance your checkbook because you don't want to know how little money you have? Whatever your fear, the only way you can overcome it is to meet it head on. Do the thing you fear, and fear will have no control over you.

- Be extra nice to someone you don't like. Pretend that you like them, and treat them accordingly. You'll be surprised at how much of your dislike for someone comes from your attitude toward them, rather than their actual behavior. Yes, perhaps a long time ago they did something that ticked you off. And ever since that time, you've been holding a grudge. You now view everything they do in terms of that grudge. That is wasted effort and energy on your part. Try liking someone and see what a difference it makes in your overall attitude. It may even make them more likable in the process.

- Do something a different way. Take a different route to the office. Eat in a restaurant where you've never eaten. Call someone you haven't spoken with for a long time. Get outside of your comfort zone and challenge yourself to think in different ways. It is easy to get into a rut, and to live our lives on "auto-pilot." You can grow only when you challenge yourself, and one of the best challenges is to put yourself in a new situation.

Try these simple steps today and see for yourself how you feel at the end of the day.

Every Moment

Every moment is an opportunity that will never come again. The things you do right now, can make a difference forever. Now is your opportunity to do what needs to be done. Now is your opportunity to become the person you want to be. Now is your opportunity to make a difference.

Right now you are creating your life. The joy, the accomplishment, the fulfillment you will achieve, come from the actions you take right now.

Look around you at the beauty of the world. Look around you at the magnificent things that you and others have already accomplished. Think of the possibilities! Think of how far you've already come. Think of how far you can go, with focus and commitment.

Make the most of each moment, and your moments will make the most of you.

12   *The Daily Motivator To Go*

I feel great today!

Try this little experiment. Wherever you're sitting, lower your head and look down. Let your shoulders droop. Say to yourself quietly "I'm really depressed. I feel awful." How do you feel?

Now try this. Sit up straight, or stand up if you want. Look up toward the sky. Put a big smile on your face and say out loud with excitement "I feel GREAT today! I am alive with excitement and enthusiasm." Now how do your feel?

Do you notice a big difference? It's all due to your physiology. By changing your posture and your voice, you have changed your attitude.

Is it realistic to say "I feel great today" when life is full of problems?

Well, you have a choice. You can choose to be depressed and despondent about your problems. You'll probably get some sympathy, but it's difficult to make your house payment with sympathy (unless you stand on the street corner with a "Will work for food" sign). Or you can choose to attack them head-on with a positive attitude. Now a positive attitude won't change your situation. But if you hold your head high and look toward the stars, you'll see a lot more opportunities than if you're looking down and depressed. You'll have more energy and more success with other people.

You're in complete control of the way you act and the way you feel. Use that to your advantage every moment.

The time to live

Time is an extremely useful tool that we have devised in order to explain and to organize the world around us. But it is only a tool. It does not define us. Our essence transcends the limiting concept of time.

If we allow ourselves to be defined by time, then we get bogged down by anger or resentment about the past, anxiety and worry about the future, and the limitations imposed by how "old" or "young" we are.

Now is the only thing we have. In that sense, there really is no such thing as time. The past and the future, while useful concepts, do not currently exist. When we become too dependent upon the past or the future, we deny ourselves the joy of the now. When we ignore the now, it escapes and does not return.

Life must be lived now. You simply cannot be successful by doing things in·the future. Plan for the future, yes, but live in the present. And no matter how great your accomplishments have been in the past, it is only by continuing to grow and seek new challenges that you remain full of life.

Treasure the past, welcome the future, and live your life in the precious moment that is now.

Ten ways to make it a great day

Do something for someone else, something unexpected, out of a sincere desire to help, with no expectation of anything in return.

Tackle a challenge that has been hanging over your head for a long time.

Try something new — a new food, a new route home, a new book, a new store.

Enjoy a few moments of quiet solitude. Think about the things in your life that are most important to you.

Call or visit a friend, just to say hello.

Learn something new, perhaps related to your job, perhaps not.

Smile for no reason at all, as often as you remember.

Say hello to a stranger.

Do something for the future, that won't "pay off" until several weeks, or months, or years from now.

When problems arise, smile and say "that's great, because..." Then find a way to finish the sentence.

The Daily Motivator To Go

Enjoy today

Whatever you find yourself doing — enjoy it. Who says that work has to be difficult and tedious? Find a way to enjoy it, and you will be infinitely more effective. Who says that cold, rainy weather has to be miserable? That's just somebody's opinion. Enjoy the cold wind on your face. Enjoy the beauty of the rainfall, and a former source of misery will change to a source of delight.

Enjoy what you do. Enjoy where you are. Enjoy the people you're with.

Too many people place limits on their happiness. "If only I could get a new job," they say, "then I'll be happy." Or "If only I could go out with her", "If only I had a new house" or "If only the weather would warm up." But when you place conditions on your enjoyment of life, then you're not really free, but rather a slave to those conditions.

When you enjoy life, you'll be better at it. It is in the things you enjoy the most, that you will find true success and effectiveness.

Make it count

Today is special. When it is over, it will be gone forever. You only have one chance to make today a productive, important one.

Each moment is an golden opportunity for you. Each moment is a chance for you to learn, to grow, to create value, to produce wealth, to make a positive difference in your own life and the lives of other people.

What you do today can improve all your tomorrows. What you do today can change the world. Today is the key. If not today, then when?

What have you always wanted? What have you always dreamed of being, doing, or having? Today is your opportunity to go for it. Today is your day to take the first step, to take positive action, to take control of your life and your future.

Today is only here once. Use it while you have it. Make it count, make it special as only you can do.

Now is the time

Now is the time to make your life count. Now is the time to live your dream. All that has happened up to this point, has prepared you. You've learned something from every experience — the good and the bad. You're strong, and capable, and effective. You can do whatever you set out to do.

Now is the time to put it all to use. Now is the time to live the life you want. Now is the time to make a difference in the world, to fulfill the enormous potential that you have always carried with you.

This is the time. There is no other. No need to wait for things to be exactly right — they're exactly right, right now. They'll never be perfect, but so what? Every moment is a precious gift, and the more of them you spend passionately in pursuit of your dream, the more fulfilled your life will be.

Now is the time. Live with everything you have.

Live at your highest level

Life is a matter of choice. Regardless of your circumstances on any particular day, you can choose the level at which you live. The person you are on the inside, is far more crucial to the quality of your life than all the outside factors combined.

This day is yours to create. Around every corner is an opportunity to live at your most effective level. Every situation and activity gives you a chance to let your highest self shine through.

This day is here, right now, and you are living it. So give it the very best you have. You're going through the motions, so why not make them count? Fill every moment with excellence by deciding to do so. Give the most you have, and you'll get back the most.

The Daily Motivator To Go

You deserve to have a wonderful life that is full of accomplishment and meaning. Choose to make it so by living today at your best.

If you don't like the weather, then change it

You can do whatever you want today.

You can walk out the door into a cold, dreary day that makes you want to go back to bed. Or you can step out into a crisp, invigorating day that puts a little extra bounce in your step. It doesn't matter what the weather report says, what matters is you.

You can get stuck in a massive traffic jam, raise your blood pressure and act rudely toward strangers. Or, you can enjoy some time for quiet reflection and find yourself amused at the hustle and bustle around you.

You can go to a terrible job, that's boring and unfulfilling, where you're not appreciated, where you have to deal with difficult people. OR, you can go to a terrific job, where you have an opportunity to make a real difference, where you're challenged to prove yourself, where you can have a positive influence on people. Both jobs are in the same building, at the same desk. The difference is all due to you.

As long as you're going through the motions, you might as well enjoy yourself and live your life to the fullest. Rather than looking for excuses to be miserable, look at each moment as an opportunity to be your best.

It's your day. It's your life. It's your choice.

The good times

When we look back on the past, we tend to remember the good times and forget about the bad times. Wouldn't it be great if we could bring that kind of positive focus to the present?

And we often don't appreciate the good things we have, until they are long gone with no hope of return.

What if you could look back from the future on where you are right now? What opportunities would you regret not following? What people would you regret not spending time with? What resources and skills would you regret wasting? What good things would you remember, and what bad things would you have forgotten?

Someday, today will be the good old days. So doesn't it make sense to make the best of every moment? Focus on the good times, and they will be.

The beauty of life

Out of the ordinary

There is nothing ordinary about life. It is the most precious thing you possess. Life is at once strong and fragile, on both counts requiring the utmost respect and consideration.

There are no ordinary moments. No matter what the circumstance, there is always, always the potential for greatness befitting the wondrous character of life itself. The difficult times, the challenges, the tragedies are all the more reason to make the most of each precious moment.

No moment is ordinary when you care, when you sincerely give of yourself, when you make the effort to make it count. Whether you're giving your child a bath, designing software, playing golf, or waiting tables, each moment is a golden opportunity. An opportunity to learn, to create, to help, to love, to fully live.

Sadness

In every life there is some sadness. The loss of a loved one, the disappointment of a shattered dream. Things don't always go the way we want.

Sadness hurts. It is difficult. And ultimately, it is good. Because sadness can come only when you care. As painful as it is, consider the alternative. What if you did not even care? Paradoxically, the absence of pain is the ultimate pain.

We must learn to experience and appreciate our sadness, without being overwhelmed by it. And the first step is to admit it and feel it for what it is. It is a powerful form of caring. About ourselves, about others, about truth, about love, about life. Sadness shows us how very much we care, and defines for us the truly important things in life.

Even in the pain of sadness, there is meaning and hope.

Out of sadness, comes a deeper sense of appreciation. The sunshine is more precious after a week of rainy days. In sadness is the strength to go forward and the opportunity to triumph over every obstacle.

A Moment of Joy

A moment of true, unencumbered joy is worth more than pure gold. You'll think more clearly, be more motivated, feel better and be healthier, when you regularly lose yourself in joy.

Not to learn. Not to look good on your résumé. Not for someone else. Not to network or impress your friends. Just for you. Simply for the experience of being fully alive and letting yourself completely enjoy yourself.

Is that selfish? No. When you have more joy in your own life, you have more to give others. By experiencing joy, you let the true person inside come to life. And that person is overflowing with love, abundance and creativity that will add immensely to your life and the lives of those around you.

Let yourself be joyful, without guilt, without expectations. You'll feel the power of that joy in every part of your life.

Beauty

What to the mind is shameful
is beauty and nothing else to the heart.
— Fyodor Dostoyevsky

Beauty cannot be truly owned, or even adequately defined. It is completely subjective, and often fleeting. It is free and it is costly. It has the ability to inspire. No one can really say what beauty is, but everyone knows it when they see it.

Beauty has its physical manifestations, but it goes far beyond the material world.

Beauty talks in the language of the heart. The magnificence of a sunset, or of a violin concerto, cannot be adequately conveyed in words. Just as food nourishes our body, beauty nourishes our spirit. It inspires and challenges us to do great things.

People of great wealth and accomplishment often surround themselves with beauty. Those who have no need or desire to impress anyone else choose to impress themselves with beauty. Perhaps, just perhaps, that's part of how they got where they are.

But you don't need to be rich or powerful to enjoy the sublime pleasure of beauty. The only thing you need is the willingness to appreciate the beauty that is already around you — in nature, in other people, in works of art, architecture, music and literature.

In a world where creativity and innovation are essential in every aspect of life, beauty is a powerful fuel for successful living.

Enjoy

True enjoyment of life can make you free.

Enjoy a glass of wine, and you are free from the need to drink the whole bottle.

Enjoy your relationships with others, and you are free from the need to control and possess them.

Enjoy the company of others, and you are free from the need to prove yourself.

Enjoy your work, and you are free to be productive.

Enjoy yourself, and you are free from guilt and anxiety.

Enjoy the challenges that come along, and you are free from being burdened with problems.

Enjoy your setbacks, and you are free to learn from them.

Enjoy your critics, and you are free to better understand yourself and others.

Enjoy your lifestyle, and you are free from the need to live beyond your means.

Enjoy a good meal, and you are free from the need to over eat.

Enjoy serving others, and you are free to know love.

Enjoy every moment, and you are free from stress and disease.

Wherever you find yourself, whatever you are doing, enjoy it. Look for good in everything, and you will find it. Enjoy what you are doing, and you'll do it better. Enjoy life, and you'll live it abundantly.

Direction and commitment

Where are you going?

Think about what you're doing now and where you're going. Most people live in a constant state of self denial. And after years and years of just barely getting by, they finally resign themselves to just that — barely getting by. They give up on their dreams. It is so sad.

But it doesn't have to be that way. You can take control of your life, of your future.

Look at what you're doing now. Is it getting you where you want to be? If not, what are you going to do about it? Are you going to keep living in a state of self denial until it's too late and you finally just completely give up on your dreams and resign yourself to an empty life of just getting by?

Or will you take control of your life. Live life to the fullest. Enjoy making a difference in the lives of others. There's nothing noble about being poor and lonely and depressed, and life does not have to be that way. Successful people are the people who help others the most That's what life's all about anyway, isn't it? We tend to forget that with all the stress and complexity of daily life, but when you stop to think about why we're all here, isn't that really it? To help each other.

When you were a child, you could imagine unlimited possibilities. You were happy and creative and you dreamed of big things. But then about the age of 6 you started getting into the "system." And gradually, little by little, every day, the system began to wear you down, to strip your dreams away, to make you conform to the mediocre standard. Your dreams are still there. They're probably buried under a thick layer of sludge, but they're still in there somewhere. Life has beaten you down, over and over again, but your dreams are still there.

Try reaching through all that and touching your dreams again. See how it feels. Imagine, just for a moment, that you can live your life to the fullest and be all you ever wanted to be and do all the things you ever wanted to do. Just imagine it for a moment.

The choice is up to you. You can continue to do what you're doing, resign yourself to a lifetime of diminished expectations, or you can grab the opportunity to be the best you can be.

Commitment

Is there something holding you back? Are things not happening for you?

Once you are committed to something, it happens. You will find a way to make it happen. Commitment is when you know that no matter how long it takes, no matter what obstacles stand in your way, no matter what, you will find a way.

Right now, you are committed to something. You're always committed to *something*. You need to ask yourself, "Is what I'm committed to really what I want?" Many people are committed to "being comfortable". This means that they will never venture out of their comfort zone. They won't do anything that might possibly make them look bad. They are so committed to comfort that they pass up opportunities, almost on a daily basis, to achieve greatness in life. It is easy to find out what you are committed to — because whatever you are committed to is probably what you have the most of. Are you committed to watching TV, so that you re-arrange your schedule around your favorite programs? Then you are probably indeed watching your favorite TV programs. Are you committed to exercise? Then you probably are in great shape. Your commitments define you.

And that's great news. Because you have complete control over your commitments. No one is forcing you to watch TV. No one is forcing you to exercise. No one is forcing you to eat junk food. No one is forcing you to get up at 5:30 every morning and review your plans for the day.

Take a good, hard look at where you are, and at what you are committed to. And if you don't like it, then decide what it is you want to change and make the commitment to that change. It will bring you all the power you need to get where you want to go.

Invest in Yourself

The harder you work
the harder it is to surrender.
— Vince Lombardi

Do you have trouble making a commitment to your goals? Perhaps you need to invest more of yourself in them. The more you work toward something, the more committed you become. And the more committed you are, the more you will work toward it. It is an upward spiral toward certain success.

Invest time and effort in yourself, and in your dreams. Start out small, and work consistently. Before you know it, you'll have something to show for your effort. And you'll have something even more important — the determination to keep going. The things you build and create, are the things you will value, appreciate, protect and use to their fullest extent.

The things you build and create, no one can take away from you. You won't let them! The goals and dreams you really work toward, no one will be able to steal from you. No amount of discouragement, challenge or setback can stop you, when you've invested enough of yourself.

Get up and get to work. Build, produce, create, take action. Then do it again and again. Before long, you won't be able to stop.

Keep going in the right direction

Do you have trouble making decisions? Is it difficult to juggle your priorities? Do you find it hard to say "no", even when you really want to? Do you sometimes sit and wonder what you should do next?

Perhaps you need to clarify your sense of direction. We all have a general idea of where we want to go, though very few people take the time to really think in specifics. But if you don't know exactly where you want to go, you tend to stray off track. Distractions come along and pull you in a lot of different directions. Decisions become difficult to make when you don't have a clear direction.

Knowing exactly where you're going can focus your efforts like nothing else. Do you ever find at the end of the day that you haven't accomplished very much? A clear sense of direction can change that.

When you know exactly where you're going, exactly what you want to do, you can use that direction to evaluate everything you do. Ask yourself, "Is what I am doing right now getting me any closer to where I want to be?" If not, then why are you doing it? If not, you'd better stop that and start doing something that will get you in the right direction.

A ship sailing across the ocean is off course 90% of the time. But because the navigator knows the final destination, he can make all the necessary course corrections along the way, before the ship gets too far off course. Those mid-course corrections are vital. And they are impossible without a specific destination.

The same holds true for any endeavor. Everything requires adjustments and corrections along the way. But in order to make the right adjustments, the final destination must be precisely defined. Only then can you keep yourself on track for success.

Vision

The biggest opportunities come to those with vision. To people who solve tough problems, who dream big dreams, who try things that have never been tried. The most successful businesses do not simply create products or services in exchange for money. They pioneer new ground. They dream big dreams and create visions so grand that people are compelled to follow them.

For the better part of the industrial age, people have been able to enjoy rising standards of living, just by learning how to use the tools of industry and by doing the jobs assigned to them. This goes for engineers, accountants, assembly line workers, technicians, salespeople, managers and most other workers. An honest day's work in the service of someone else's vision, in return for good pay.

That is all changing. Technology is providing the leverage that once was supplied by a well-run corporation. The result is that one individual, properly equipped, can do the work of hundreds. All of a sudden, the dreamers and the visionaries no longer need all the dedicated employees.

Too many people have become too good at using the tools of production, and no good at figuring out what to do with those tools. For the most part, we were not taught in school to be creative — we were taught to be productive. We've concentrated all our lives on the "how" and never thought about the "why."

To prosper in the coming information age, we must become masters of the "why." We must dare to dream big dreams, to explore uncharted territory, to develop new concepts and follow our vision. For the person who can do that, there is infinite opportunity. Look around you. For everything you see, ask yourself "why?", "why not?" and "what if?" You'll see opportunity in every direction.

Don't depend solely on your competence, or your expertise, or your specialized knowledge to carry you through life.

Look inside yourself and find a vision. Find a "why" and you'll suddenly see a lifetime of opportunity.

Finding your vision

How do you find the "why" for your life? It is really very easy. You find a why by asking "why?"

Think of something you want. Chances are the first thing you think of will be something material. That's OK, there's nothing wrong with that. Just make sure it is something you really want, not something you say you want just because you think you should. I'm going to use, as an example, a boat. Not just any boat, but a 50 foot sailing yacht with seaworthy rigging and a big, comfortable living space.

Next step: ask yourself why. Why do I want this boat? To sail to the South Pacific.

Again, ask yourself why. Why do I want to sail to the South Pacific? Hmmm. Let's see. I've always wanted to do it, but I just kind of took it for granted. I guess because it would be an exciting adventure.

And again, ask why. Why do I want an exciting adventure? Well, that's getting kind of tough. I want an exciting adventure because I want to experience life to the fullest.

Fair enough. That's a good reason. And why do I want to experience life to the fullest? Whew, this is getting a little intense. I want to experience life to the fullest because I am fascinated by the possibilities that life offers. Fascinated? Well, OK, I admit it. I'm obsessed with the possibilities that life offers.

Now we're getting somewhere. And why am I obsessed with the possibilities that life offers?

The answer: *because that's me*. Bingo! We're there. We've asked "why" enough times that we've gotten down to the ultimate why. And that, by the way, is mine, as nearly as I can determine it, though the example given is not the way I arrived at it. I am driven by possibilities. That is my why.

How will you know it when you reach yours? Trust me, you'll know it. It will be a very emotional experience when you get to the basic why of your life. And a very empowering experience. Because once you've been there, so many things will become clear. You'll see things you never knew that you never knew. You'll gain a deeper, clearer understanding of yourself and your place in the world, and an appreciation of what your life has to offer.

Find success by doing what you love

You just won't find anyone who has achieved massive success by doing something that they hate. To achieve success, you must find something that you absolutely love to do. Something that you cannot, *not* do. And do it well. Do it with passion, with excitement, with enthusiasm, with a healthy obsession.

That is not to say that you must become a workaholic. Because when you find something that you absolutely love to do, it's not work. It's fun. Obsession with making money creates workaholics. Focusing on limitation creates workaholics. Don't focus on making money, because then you'll be working. Focus instead on creating your dream job, on doing what you love to do the most. The money will come, but it is only one measure of your success. More importantly, you'll grow as a person. You'll grow into the person you were meant to be. You will fulfill your potential and make your unique contribution to the world. And that is worth far more than any check that anyone could write to you.

Mark Twain said, "The secret of success is making your vocation your vacation." Successful people are on a permanent vacation. Not because they don't work hard, but because they love what they do.

The other night on the radio a caller to a talk show was asked, "What would you do if you won the lottery?" Her reply was that she would "never work another day in my life." It always makes me very sad to hear something like that. It is sad to think that there are people who hate what they are doing. They'll never get anywhere with an attitude like that. And it is sad to think that the ultimate goal in life would be to NOT work. Can you imagine anything more empty? Think for a moment how that would be — never contributing anything of value.

If your goal is to get to the point where you never have to work again, perhaps you should examine the nature of your work. Hating what you do will probably not get you very far. Find a way to love your work and you'll immediately have true success.

Enjoying what you do

I have a book in my library titled *Do What You Love, The Money Will Follow.* At the time I bought the book, the "money will follow" part served to give me some degree of reassurance. I've since come to realize that it is becoming increasingly difficult to make a living any other way.

As our world becomes more sophisticated, and as technology replaces more and more jobs, the world of work is changing dramatically. It seems that no one, no matter what their skill level, is immune from job cutbacks and corporate re-engineering. The hard, cold fact is that cheap, powerful computers can replace much of the work done by humans, even highly trained humans. This applies to doctors, lawyers, managers and engineers just as much as it applies to factory workers and filing clerks.

There is one thing, however, that computers will never be able to replace. And that is passion. And as computers take over more and more of the work done by humans, the need for passion will be greater and greater. Why is this? Because computers and other automated systems are excellent at carrying out tasks assigned to them. They can fabricate, design, manufacture, distribute, price, analyze, and do all sorts of

The Daily Motivator To Go

other logical, necessary things. To do all these things, however, they need to have a goal. They need to be told what to do. And only humans can do that. Because only humans can know, with passion, what other humans need.

Computers cannot write great stories. They cannot appreciate beauty. Computers have no passion. And that's where we come in.

In the years to come, the most successful people will be those who embrace technology and use it to express their human passions. We need dreamers, and we are willing to pay them well. Look at the success of the Walt Disney Company which has as it's publicly perceived mission statement, "when you wish upon a star... your dreams come true." That may sound like childish and naive, but it equals billions of dollars in the bank. This is a company that embraced communication technology more than 50 years ago and used it to help people explore their own human passions.

In the high tech world that is taking shape right before our eyes, it is absolutely crucial that you enjoy what you do for a living. Because your value in the marketplace depends on it. Your skills and your expertise may very well be replaced or re-engineered out of significance. Your dreams and your passions, however, can never be replaced. When you enjoy what you do, you put the whole of your person into it. Your work takes on a value that cannot be duplicated. You make a unique and significant contribution, adding value to everything you do.

If you don't enjoy what you do for a living, then you have two choices: find something else that you do enjoy, or find a way to enjoy what you do. As you prepare your work skills for the years ahead, passion is one you do not want to ignore.

Little choices - big results

Today you will face countless choices. They may each seem insignificant, but they're not. Most of them, you probably won't even think about — you'll make these choices by habit. Others, you'll consider briefly, perhaps, and then move on to something else.

We tend to focus on the "big" choices: where to go to college, what house to buy, who to marry, what career to choose. And these are important decisions. Yet the little choices — the ones you make every day without even thinking — add up over the months and years to have a huge impact on your life. The cumulative effect of these little choices is powerful indeed.

Let's say you choose at lunch to have a double-meat cheeseburger, large order of onion rings and a piece of cheesecake, instead of having a green salad and a bowl of fresh fruit. It won't make much difference today which you choose. However, over the course of a year, your daily choice of food can make a tremendous difference in your health and fitness.

Other choices that you make every day: To spend 10 minutes circling and fighting for a parking space next to the building, or to park out where there are plenty of spaces and spend 3 minutes walking across the parking lot. To call a friend or to watch another re-run of "Coach". To assign blame or to solve the problem. To do something the way it's always been done, or to look for a new approach. To pay someone a compliment, or to mind your own business. To take off early, or to work a few minutes late. These choices combine to form your life. In what direction are your choices taking you?

The life you live right now is a result of the choices you have made in the past. Be aware of your choices every day. Take control of your life with the choices you make, especially the "little" ones.

Are you living the life you choose?

Ask yourself: are you living the life you choose? The answer is...

Yes!

Because what you are, what you have, and what you do are all the result of choices you have made. You are where you are right now because of what you have chosen. If you don't like where you are, you can waste a lot of time, effort and energy blaming someone or something for your situation. We all have obstacles, though, and success in life is based primarily on whether we chose to see those obstacles as excuses or as challenges. It makes all the difference in the world.

Your life is determined by your choices. You can chose to sit around all night watching TV, or you can choose to spend your evening enriching your mind, perhaps learning a new skill. You can choose to dull your senses with drugs and alcohol, or you can choose to keep your body in top shape with challenging exercise. You can choose to stand quietly in the corner at the party, or to use it as an opportunity to meet interesting people.

Surprisingly, the important choices aren't the big ones. It is the cumulative effect of the little choices that makes the biggest difference. We may agonize for weeks or months over what school to attend, what career to pursue or what job offer to accept. These are what we consider big, important choices. In reality, though, our life is determined more by the "little" choices that we make every day: Should I make that extra phone call? Should I volunteer for that project? Should I introduce myself to the new department manager? Should I have another piece of cheesecake? Should I roll over and sleep for another 20 minutes? Should I watch that re-run of Sienfeld for the 4th time?

Choices, not chances, determine our destiny. What do you choose?

Invest in the future

Fast food. Instant coffee. Overnight delivery. Microwave ovens. Faxes. E-mail. Everywhere you look there is technology for instant gratification. We've come to expect immediate results. There's certainly nothing wrong with having a sense of urgency — that's the way we get things done. However, some of the best things in life simply take time.

The more you invest in the future, the better it will be. Sure, you want to put plenty of energy into living for today. But today turns all too soon into yesterday. And when you suddenly find yourself in what used to be the future, it helps when you've sent some energy ahead.

Investing in the future will make time your friend, and give you a reason to look forward to each new day.

Do something that will bring you instant gratification, and it's gone at the end of the day. Do something today that won't benefit you for six months, and suddenly your future is brighter. The farther into the future you plan and work, the greater your influence will be when your effort comes to fruition.

Make a habit of planting seeds each day, and the future will bring a bountiful harvest.

Learn to say NO

It may sound strange, but one of the most positive things you can do is to say "No" when necessary. The ability to say "No" is directly proportional to your confidence in yourself and your belief in what you are doing.

You must be able to say "No" in order to stay focused. There are too many distractions that come along, too many people vying for your time. If you don't learn to say "No", you get spread too thin. Of course you don't want to miss any big opportunities, but neither can you be all things to all people.

You can have anything you want, but you can't have everything you want. You can't be a doctor and a lawyer and a scientist and an engineer and an airline pilot. You have to make choices, and that means saying "yes" to some things and "no" to others.

A sincere, honest "No" shows that you have the courage of your convictions, and that you are committed to staying on track. And what's so hard about it, anyway? It's just a word. Learn to say it, politely and firmly (No, thank you), with compassion and conviction, and you'll take control of your own destiny.

Where there's a will...

The willingness to do something creates the ability to do it. If you are willing enough to get something done, it will get done. Don't spend too much time worrying about how it will be done. You'll find a way if you're willing.

Your willingness can summon enormous resources within yourself and without, to bring about what you want.

So how do you create this powerful desire within yourself?

By knowing why. When you truly understand why you want something, you'll have the willingness required to get it. And if you can't find a why, then you really don't want it in the first place.

You can use willingness to turn around any negative, limiting thoughts that might creep into your mind. Just add the phrase "but I'm willing to" and you instantly turn a negative into a positive, like this:

I'm really not comfortable making sales calls...

...but I'm willing to give it my best shot.

I don't know how to do this...

...but I'm willing to learn.

I'm discouraged that I lost the business...

...but I'm willing to keep on trying until I succeed.

Be willing to do whatever it takes to succeed, and you will.

You can do it

You have the power and the ability to be whatever you want to be, to do whatever you want to do, to have whatever you want to have.

Look at all the things that people have done — built great fortunes, created great works of art, developed incredibly powerful machines, influenced millions with their words. The list is endless. There is no limit to accomplishment.

You were born to do great things. Every human accomplishment has been attained by someone just like you. Everything that has ever been possible, is possible for you. Whatever you can imagine, is possible for you. Yes, for you. If you are willing to take action. If you are willing to do what needs to be done.

Are there obstacles? Yes, of course there are. Nothing worthwhile comes easy. In fact, it is precisely the struggle and the challenge that makes anything valuable.

Right now, today, you have a choice. You can sit back, complain about how unfair life is, make excuses for not ever doing anything, and watch the world pass you by. OR you can stand up, step forward, boldly take on each challenge that comes your way, and do whatever it takes to make something of your life.

The journey

You arrive at the airline ticket counter with your bags packed and ready. You pull out a billfold full of cash, and say to the ticket agent, "I'd like a ticket, please."

"Certainly," says the agent. "Where would you like to go?"

"Someplace nice. Where I can have a good job, make plenty of money, drive a new car, live in a big house, and have a lot of friends," you answer.

"And exactly where would that be?" asks the agent.

"I'm not sure just yet," you reply. "But once I get going, I should have a better idea."

"I'm sorry," says the agent. "You obviously have enough

money for a ticket to anywhere you wish to travel. However, in order to issue a ticket, I'll need to know exactly where you intend to go. If you don't know that, I'll have to ask you to step aside. Next, please."

The person behind you steps up to the counter. "I'd like a ticket to Paris," he announces.

"Certainly," says the agent. "And how will you be paying for this?"

"I'm not sure just yet," he answers. "But once I get going I should be able think of a way."

"I'm sorry," replies the agent. "But I cannot issue a ticket without your payment. Next, please."

A successful journey has two essential requirements: a clear destination, and the means to get there. Your goals and dreams are the destination of your life journey. Your discipline and effort are the means of travel. Without one, the other is wasted. With both, you can go wherever you want to be.

Stick With It

I wonder how many people give up on their dream when they are just a week or two away from the big breakthrough that would bring it about?

One of the most challenging aspects of attaining success is to maintain a sense of urgency about your work, while at the same being patient enough to stick with it for as long as necessary.

It takes belief, faith and confidence.

Belief in what you are doing. Faith that the value you are creating will eventually come back to you, multiplied many times over. Confidence that comes from knowing that you are putting forth your very best effort.

If you work on something long enough, sincerely giving your best effort every day, constantly looking for ways to improve your performance and the value that you bring to the work, and it will succeed.

The most worthwhile accomplishments take time. That doesn't mean you can sit back and wait for them. Because they also require aggressive pursuit on a daily basis. Know where you're going, do your best work, give it everything you possibly can, provide as much value to as many people as possible, every opportunity you get, and then know with confidence that your efforts will be richly rewarded.

Nobel's Wake Up Call

One morning Alfred Nobel, the Swedish chemist who made a fortune from his invention of dynamite, awoke to find his own obituary printed in the newspaper. The newspaper story had been a mistake, of course. But after reading it, Nobel realized that he didn't want to be known for giving society the ability to blow things up. Instead, he wanted to leave a legacy that promoted peace, culture and science.

So he set aside the majority of his multi-million dollar fortune to fund annual prizes for exceptional achievement in physics, chemistry, medicine, literature, and world peace. Today, a hundred years after his death, few people realize that Alfred Nobel was the inventor of dynamite, yet almost everyone has heard of the Nobel Prizes.

Alfred Nobel was fortunate enough to read his own obituary while he still had the opportunity to change the focus of his life. And as a result, his efforts continue to benefit mankind to this day.

We often get so caught up in the day-to-day, urgent details of life. Yet in all our getting and doing, we need to regularly step back and look at the big picture. It can often make a significant difference.

What does success mean to you?

Right now, you are 100% successful, when measured against your own definition of success. Whatever you are, whatever you have, whatever you're doing now — these are the things you've set your sights on achieving. These are the things you've committed to with your behavior and your actions.

If your definition of success is to sit in front of the TV with a beer, then that's probably what you're doing, and your lifestyle reflects it. You may not think of that as "successful". Yet whatever you've set as your priority, is your own true personal definition of success.

It is almost impossible for you not to attain the goals to which you are truly committed.

You've been completely successful at designing and achieving the life you now live. If you're not happy with that life, all you need to do is change your own definition of success. Change it, that is, not just in your thoughts and words, but in your actions, in your commitments.

You have what it takes to be successful at anything. Already, your priorities have been successfully manifest in the life you now live. You can have any life you want, when you adopt the necessary priorities.

What will it take?

What will it take to get where you really want to go? To have the things you really want to have? To be the person you really want to be?

What will it take?

It will take work. Hard work. Late nights. Frustration. Sacrifice. Discipline. Effort. Disappointment. Discomfort. It will take your total commitment. It will take the best that you have to give.

If you think that sounds tough, consider the alternative. Regret. Wondering what you could have done if only you had given it your best shot. The waste of a life half lived, and you can't go back.

So the choice is up to you: an easy path with a heartbreaking destination, or a challenging path with a destination of fulfillment and joy.

Any way you cut it, life is difficult. But is that really so bad? It is in the challenges that we grow. It is in overcoming the difficulties that we find our greatest accomplishments. Face life head-on, deal with the challenges as they come. Accept that life is difficult, quit wishing or pretending that it is easy, and you will then be free to live with joy and purpose and fulfillment.

Positive expectations

On top of the world

Imagine for a moment that you're on top of the world today — that everything is going your way, that nothing can get you down.

You're enthusiastic about your work, and effective in getting things done. You're polite, considerate and respectful toward others — a real joy to be around. You're full of great ideas, and have the energy to pursue them.

You see the good in everything that happens. The day is filled with opportunity. You delight in the beauty that is around you, and appreciate the abundance that is in your life.

You're confident in your posture and your speech. You meet every challenge that comes along with a calm self assurance. You feel great. You like the person you are, and so does everyone else.

Now, stop imagining and start doing. Live today like you're on top of the world, and you will be.

Expect the Best

Expect the best from life and you'll generally get it.

Your expectations play a key role in the reality of your life. Your mind is a powerful goal-seeking device. When you point it in the right direction, with positive expectations, it will do whatever is necessary to get you where you want to go. The more consistently you keep your mind on your positive expectations, the faster they will become a reality.

Expect the best of those around you, and you generally will get it. Think for a moment what would happen if you bought something at the store and later found out it was defective. When you return to the store for a refund or a replacement, you have two choices. You could choose to expect a hard time.

That is, you could go into the store with the expectation that you're going to have to fight with them to get a refund. And if you approach them with that attitude, you probably will have to exchange some harsh words with the store clerk. Your other choice is to expect the best. Assume that they will be eager to satisfy you. Approach them with that attitude. And when you do that, they probably will be very eager to set you straight and issue a refund.

Nowhere does this principle apply more than with children. When you nag and complain to your children all day long about how naughty they are, guess what? Their behavior will get worse and worse. When you expect the best of them, and give them responsibility and respect, they will immediately sense it and their behavior will improve almost overnight.

Are you having problems dealing with someone — a family member, a business associate, a neighbor? Have you come to the point where you expect the worst of them? Do they generally live up to that expectation? Realize that your expectation has become a large part of the problem. What do you think would happen if you started treating them as if you liked and respected them? You don't have to really like them or approve of what they're doing. You don't have to back down from your position. Just treat them and relate to them as if you completely respect them as a person. Expect the best from them, and just see what happens.

More than anything, expect the best from yourself. Talk to yourself in positive terms. Don't say "if I get a new house." Say "when I get a new house." Don't say "I'll try to build my business." Say "I am building my business." Words like "try" and "if" presuppose a negative outcome. In other words, you have to accept the possibility of failure in order for these words to make sense. That may not sound like such a big deal, and it isn't when you only do it once or twice. The thing is, you are constantly talking to yourself. Your thought patterns reinforce your expectations, over and over again, all day long, day after day after day. The least little bit of negativity, repeated again and again, can build itself into an invisible wall of negative expectations.

Learn to expect the best from yourself. In the way you talk to yourself, in the way you plan for the future, in the choices you make. Ask yourself, as often as possible, what you would do if you were truly headed in the direction of your goals. And then just do it.

Positive Expectations

You are what you expect of yourself, what you think of yourself.

If you're a golfer who usually shoots in the mid-90s, and you shoot a 39 on the first nine holes, then you'll likely compensate with a lousy performance on the back nine to finish up at your usual score. If you're salesperson earning $120,000 a year and you lose your job, chances are you'll find another job that earns you around $120,000 a year.

Success is often hindered by nothing more than low expectations. You may have the best education, an impressive list of contacts, skills, experience and a growing market — but if you don't see yourself as succeeding, you won't.

Every day, you talk to yourself more than you talk to anyone else. Your inner voice is constantly advising you and reminding you. What is it saying? Is it saying "Yes, you can do this" or is it saying "there's no way you can do this?" The difference is crucial. And the good news is, you can change that inner voice. All it takes is a commitment to expect more of yourself. In an instant, you can change your expectations from negative to positive.

See it and you'll be it

Visualization plays a key role in your life, whether you realize it or not. What you constantly visualize and think about is generally what you become.

If you are always dwelling on the negative — your health problems, the money you owe, your troubled relationships — then you give even more power to these things and they continue to manifest in your life in abundance.

By contrast, when you constantly visualize life the way you want it to be — optimum health, increased income, free of debt — then these things will begin to appear.

It almost seems like magic, but there is nothing magical about it. Our minds work by association. There is so much information coming at us on a daily basis that we can't possibly process it all. So we experience life and relate to the world in terms of things we already know. You create a model in your mind that allows you to make sense of the world around you.

When that model is positive, and focused on your goals, then you see the opportunities in all situations. Make a habit of constantly focusing on the positive and visualizing the person you want to become. When you regularly visualize yourself as successful and effective, then your mind will find a way to bring that visualization into reality.

Something to look forward to

Have you ever noticed what happens right before you're going on a long-awaited vacation? If you're like most people, you are bulletproof. Nothing gets you down. You cheerfully work harder than usual to get things ready for your trip, and to arrange for everything to continue smoothly while you are gone. In fact, for many people, the day before leaving on vacation is often the most productive day they have all year.

Why is that? Well, for one thing, you HAVE to get the work done. You have a sense of urgency. It won't wait until tomorrow. So you're extremely motivated in that regard. You also have a "light at the end of the tunnel." You know that tomorrow you'll be relaxing on the beach, or hiking through the mountains, and that is enough to keep you going at a high level of energy and enthusiasm.

Wouldn't it be great if every day could be like that? Just think how much you would accomplish.

When you think about it, the day before vacation is no different than any other day. The only thing that makes it different is your attitude. Guess what? You're in complete control of your attitude. So... if you really want, you can feel that way every day.

The trick is to find something exciting and inspiring to look forward to. Yes, a vacation is great, but you can't do that every day. That's where your goals come into play.

What is your life's dream? What excites you, and motivates you, and inspires you more than anything else? Whatever it is, you need to constantly remind yourself of it. Keep it at the front of your mind. Know that everything you are doing is leading to that goal.

Goals aren't really important for what they are, so much as for what they help you to become. In fact, reaching your goal is not nearly as important as what you do, and what you become, in the process. We are goal seeking creatures. We need something to strive for, to look forward to. Provide that for yourself, and every day can be joyous and productive.

Think about it

Whatever you dwell upon, grows. The more emotionally and intensely you think about it and concentrate on it, the more it grows and expands. What do you think about?

Do you constantly think about your problems? Then they will increase. Instead, dwell upon your goals. You can only hold one thought in your mind at a time. So get in the habit of substituting positive thoughts for negative ones.

That is why goals are so important. They give you something positive to focus on. When you continually think about your goals, there's simply no room left for negative thoughts.

You subconscious mind is a powerful resource that can work

for you or against you. The subconscious mind makes no judgments — it simply carries out the orders sent to it by the conscious mind. When you focus on the positive things that you want to achieve, when you repeatedly visualize them in detail, you are sending commands to your subconscious mind. Once you've given it a clear direction, your subconscious will find a way to bring your goals into reality.

Constantly think positive thoughts.

The power of·thought

Your thoughts become your reality. All behavior comes from the thoughts that preceded it. Every accomplishment great and small begins with a thought, a vision.

When you control your own thoughts, and focus them on a specific set of goals, then you have taken full control of your life. You are no longer a victim of circumstance, the moment you begin to visualize your own future.

No one can control your thoughts except you. No one can influence your thoughts unless you let them. Choose carefully the people who would affect your thinking. Surround yourself with positive, responsible, intelligent, open-minded thinking.

The person you are on the inside determines the person you become on the outside. Your mind, your body, and the whole world that surrounds you, are crying out for direction, waiting to be shaped and guided by your thoughts. Waiting to leverage your thoughts into manifestation.

Think about the person you want to become, because you become the person you think about.

Belief

During the first half of this century, scientists, physicians, athletes and trainers believed that it was impossible for a human to run a mile in less than four minutes. People had tried unsuccessfully for decades to break this barrier. The conventional wisdom held that the human body was physiologically incapable of running at this pace — that the cardiovascular and skeletal systems simply would break down before the four-minute barrier was crossed.

Then, on May 6, 1954, Roger Bannister ran a mile in 3 minutes, 59.4 seconds. He did this because he believed he could. And once he had done it, everyone else suddenly believed it could be done, too. Within 3 years, another runner had broken the four-minute barrier. Now, there are thousands of people who have run a mile in under four minutes.

For over one hundred years, runners had tried unsuccessfully to break the four-minute barrier. Then, after one person had done it, thousands more were able to do it. Did the physiology of the human body suddenly change? No, of course not. The thing that changed was belief. People replaced a limiting belief (under four minutes is impossible) with an empowering belief.

What beliefs do you have? Do they limit you or do they lift you up? Whatever you truly believe is possible, is.

To be a winner you must think like a winner

If you believe you can do a thing,
or you believe you can not,
you're probably right.
            — Henry Ford

Did you know that your mind "thinks" about 60,000 thoughts every day? Just by the sheer volume of them, your thoughts have a huge impact on your life.

Whether you think you can or you think you can't, you're right. Everything you do begins in your mind. Success is an inside job. You can choose to think empowering thoughts or you can settle for limiting thoughts. You can think the same old thoughts over and over again, or you can expose yourself to new experiences, concepts and possibilities. It's completely up to you and the way you choose to think.

Look for the opportunities in every situation. Constantly think to yourself, "I can do it." Use those 60,000 thoughts to program yourself for success. When you believe in what you're doing, and believe that you can do it, you'll find a way to make it happen.

The things that regularly occupy your thinking, have the power to drive your life. Your mind is too powerful to ignore. Take control of your thoughts and you will have control of your destiny.

Expectations

Elephants have been trained and used by humans as work animals for as long as 4,000 years. How is it possible for a 175 pound man to keep an 11,000 pound elephant in captivity?

When an elephant is very young, it is tethered to a four foot long wooden stake driven into the ground. This stake is physically able to hold the young, small elephant, despite the elephant's repeated attempts to escape it. After unsuccessfully trying many times to escape, the young elephant eventually comes to believe that escape is impossible. This belief is carried into adulthood. When the elephant is full grown, it could easily break free from the four-foot wooden stake, yet it never even attempts to do so. This intelligent, powerful creature is held captive, not by any physical restraint, but by its own thoughts.

Does it make you wonder what thoughts of your own might be holding you back? Are you tethered to circumstances from which you could easily break free, if only you knew you could?

Your thoughts can be your prison, or they can set you free to soar. If you think you can, or if you think you can't, you're absolutely right. In order to do anything, or become anything, or have anything, you must first believe that it is possible. It must exist in your mind before it can come to pass.

Expectations become reality, so expect the best of yourself.

48   *The Daily Motivator To Go*

Talk like a winner

Your behavior is strongly influenced by the things you say, think and feel. Your words, thoughts and feelings affect each other, and also affect your actions.

If you're like most people, the easiest of these to control is what you say. And by changing the way you express things, you can actually improve your performance and effectiveness. Studies have found that optimistic people perform at a higher level than pessimists. Optimists look at a situation and see benefits, opportunities and learning experiences. Pessimists look at the same situation and see only the risks.

The fact is that most people talk, in everyday life, in negative terms. It's so common that few people even realize they're doing it. "How's it going?" someone asks. "Not bad," is the reply. "What are you doing?" "Not much."

For a change, try this: "How's it going?" "Great!" "What are you doing?" "I'm enjoying life." Notice how much better that feels. It seems silly and insignificant, yet make it a habit and it will quickly change your outlook. Try saying "I'm enjoying life" five times. How do you feel?

Or look at how we commonly persuade: "Why don't we go to the ball game tonight?" Stated in the negative, this literally makes you start thinking of reasons why NOT to go to the ball game. Listen to how much better this sounds: "Let's go to the ball game tonight."

A few other examples:

"If you decide to do business with us, your order won't be delayed."

"When you decide to do business with us, we'll ship immediately."

In this case, "If" presumes that they might NOT do business. "When" presumes that they will.

"I understand what you're saying, but we won't let you down."

"I understand what you're saying, and we can handle that."

Look at the enormous difference in confidence and credibility, just by changing a few words.

Language is powerful. Practice making it a positive force in your life.

I could never...

Do you ever catch yourself saying "I could never..."? I could never quit my job, tell him the truth, speak in front of a large group, make a parachute jump, ask her for a date, learn to speak another language, shoot below 90, play the guitar like that. I could never do that.

Why not? What do you mean, "I could never"? Of course you could. You could indeed. If it can be done, you can do it. You've got to want it, of course. And if you want it enough, you'll do it.

"I could never" is usually said wistfully, meaning "I wish I could, but I can't." That's preposterous. You can if you want to. Free yourself from your own limitations. What do you want to do? What will fulfill the enormous potential of your life? Certainly not hiding behind "I could never."

You are capable of truly extraordinary accomplishments. You can do whatever you decide you're going to do. You can find a way. Have the courage to live your possibilities.

What you see is what you get

Is the glass half full, or half empty? It's a classic conundrum that drives home a powerful point — you see what you choose to see.

Two sales agents were sent to sell shoes in an underdeveloped third world nation. The first agent sent a message back to his office, "No prospect of sales because nobody wears shoes here." The other sales agent sent a different message, "Send stock immediately. Inhabitants barefooted. Desperately need shoes." Looking at the same "reality", each person saw a completely different situation.

We all have the same five senses. Yet the sensory input that we receive must be interpreted before we can understand and act on it. Though we often cannot control the reality of the world, we have complete control over our perception and interpretation of reality. And we have complete control over the actions we take in response. And it is that perception, and those actions, that make all the difference in life.

Everyone's alarm clock sounds basically the same. Only to the successful person, however, is it the sound of opportunity. What does your alarm clock sound like?

Everyone's copy of the daily newspaper contains the same articles. However, only the copy that lands in the successful person's driveway has stories of unlimited possibilities.

You can literally program yourself for success by changing the way you perceive the world around you. You will find what you look for. The so-called "reality" of the outside world is only a mirror. A mirror which confirms and gives evidence to the vision that you have on the inside.

The world is what you expect it to be, and nothing else. Expect the best and that is the kind of world you will create.

What do you expect?

What do you expect to be doing next week? Six months from now? Five years from now? I'm not really talking about goals, or new year's resolutions. Rather, what do you really expect you'll be doing?

If you want the best out of life, you must expect the best. Because whatever you expect of yourself, whatever you expect for yourself, is what you will get.

Expectation is not the same as wishing. You can wish for a million dollars, you can even convince yourself that it will somehow fall into your hands. Yet if wishing is all you do, it won't happen. On the other hand, if you truly expect to be a millionaire, and if that expectation pervades all of your actions on a daily basis, then you'll find yourself doing whatever it takes, for as long as it takes, to make your expectation a reality.

True expectations influence every area of your life, and that is how they work their magic. You can work hard for 10 hours every day, and if you just expect to barely get by, that's what will happen. Work those same 10 hours with the expectation of getting wealthy, and suddenly you'll find all sorts of opportunities and possibilities that you never would have seen before.

What you expect, makes all the difference.

Just suppose

Why do you feel so joyful today? What makes you so effective and successful in the things you do? How do you know exactly the right thing to do? What is it that keeps you so positively focused?

How do you feel after reading the above questions? Pretty great, huh? These questions are phrased as presuppositions. In order to make sense of them, you must first assume that they are true. "Why do you feel so joyful today?" There's no way to even think that thought without believing that you are joyful today.

Unfortunately, most of us think in negative suppositions. "Why can I never make ends meet?" "What makes me fail every time?" These work the same way. When we ask these questions, we are forced to believe the negative assumptions.

Take a look at the questions you ask yourself. They determine your focus. They determine your beliefs about yourself. Just imagine what could happen if you started asking yourself things such as: "What can I learn from this?" "How can I make the most of this situation?" "What is right about my life?"

Focus on the positive by assuming the best and you'll see opportunity everywhere you look.

Act as if

How would you act today if your were totally confident, highly successful, happy and fulfilled in your life? How would you walk, how would you sit, how would you talk, how would you work?

Imagine yourself acting as if you had it all — success, effectiveness, confidence and fulfillment. And then do it. Walk the way you would walk if you were a smashing success. Talk the way you would talk if you were totally confident. Enjoy every moment the way you would if you were completely fulfilled.

Now, realize this. When you take successful actions, you are successful. When you act confidently, you are confident. When you live out fulfillment, you are fulfilled. Your actions determine your reality.

Act as if you already had it, and before long, you will.

Quality of Life

The quality of your life is determined by the quality of your thoughts and the quality of your actions.

If your thoughts are petty, cynical and vindictive, your life will be filled with frustration and regret. If the actions you take are the minimum needed to get by, the you'll always be just barely getting by.

When your thoughts are positive and expansive, your actions bold and determined, you will live with abundance and fulfillment.

Quality of life is not based so much on what you have. Rather, it depends on how you choose to view, and what you choose to do. Think of every moment as an opportunity. Act with purpose, direction, enthusiasm and commitment. Every little thought, every little action, combines to determine the quality of your life. Every day is a chance to create, by what you think and what you do, the best person you can be.

Goals and dreams

Dig out your dreams and dust them off

What is your dream? More than anything else, what do you want to accomplish in your life? And why?

We get so caught up in the day-to-day activities, the "overhead" of life, that we usually forget to seek out and appreciate the real substance of life. What is your dream? Do you know?

Yes, you have one. You've probably had it since you were a child. When we're children, dreams come easy. Anything is possible and we're not limited by the narrow-mindedness that experience brings. Every child has dreams.

And then "reality" sets in. Responsibility. Decisions. Trying to please and impress other people. Little by little, as we grow older, the world begins to cover our dreams over. Layer upon layer of sludge and debris get piled on top of our dreams until finally we no longer know they're there.

But they are. They're buried deep, but your dreams are there. And occasionally you connect with them, if only for a second. You see something, hear something, catch a whiff of a scent from long ago. Your dream comes back to you for a moment and you feel a deep sense of regret that you never did follow it. Then something "more important" comes along and it's gone again.

What are you living for if not to follow your dreams? Are you living for money? Are you living for pleasure? Have you taken the easy way out and allowed yourself to live for someone else's dream?

Dig down deep and connect with your life's dreams. Have a dream and you'll have a life that's full and rewarding.

The Daily Motivator To Go

See where you're going

Success in life comes from consistently working toward your goals. This means staying on track on the "bad" days as well as the "good" days.

You've got to see each event in your life, not as an isolated activity, but rather as another link in the chain that leads to your ultimate goal. This will put each day in perspective for you. Things don't always go well, there are setbacks and frustrations along the way. And the key phrase is "along the way."

Realize that each day, no matter what happens, you are that much closer to your goal. Each sale made, each report written, each lesson learned is not just an isolated event — it is another step in the direction that you have chosen for yourself.

Make a habit of looking all the way to the end of the chain. Look at how much closer you've gotten today. Look at what is coming up tomorrow. Look at the next steps for which you must begin preparation. Look all the way and see yourself getting closer.

And... enjoy the journey. You're in control of your life, you have purpose and direction. Realize that wherever you are along the path, fulfillment is already yours.

Think ahead, Work ahead, Be ahead

What will tomorrow be like? Well, that's a very good question. The answer depends primarily on what you do today. Tomorrow will be like... whatever you plan and work for it to be. The same goes for next week, next month, next year, and so on.

If you don't really have a plan, then tomorrow will be left to chance. You'll drift along with whatever comes by. There's nothing wrong with that, if you like drifting. But if you want more direction, if you have something you'd like to do, or be, or have tomorrow, then you need to start planning and working for it today.

Here's something to remember — the further ahead you plan, the more control you have. Take, for example, flying on a commercial airline. If you show up at the airport, with no ticket, 30 minutes before the flight is leaving, you'll be lucky just to get a seat, and you'll pay the airline's highest fare. If, however, you plan your trip 3 months in advance, you get your choice of seat, you can often even choose your in-flight meal, and you can probably get a substantial discount on the fare.

Why do airlines reward you for planning ahead? Because it enables them to plan ahead and to allocate their resources in the most efficient and effective manner. Why should you plan ahead in all areas of your life? Same reason — so you can make the very most of what you have.

Think ahead. What will be happening in 3 months, 6 months, 2 years? You'll have to deal with the details eventually, so why not start dealing with them now? Planning ahead always gives you more options, plus you'll get more for the money or effort involved.

What can you do today to make tomorrow go more smoothly? What can you do today to make next week more productive? How can you act today to make your life better one month from now? Or 6 months from now? Or 5 years? Think about it. And get started today, right now, on a better tomorrow.

Listen to your own dream

Life is too short to spend it living someone else's dream. Listen to yourself. Really listen. What will make your life meaningful and fulfilling?

It's easy to let someone else make all your decisions for you — when to show up for work, when to go home, what to do with your day, when to go to lunch and for how long, what to wear, how much money you will make, how much vacation time you'll get. That's the easy way out.

Reaching for a better life is not easy. It is uncomfortable. It takes courage, determination, commitment and action. Is it worth all that? You bet!

You have one life to live. Do you want to spend that life just getting by? Or do you want to make your own unique contribution to the world? The choice is yours. Life is wonderful and precious. Find what you want out of life and live it all the way.

Make your goals real

It's easy to set goals for yourself. Yet they are meaningless if you don't really believe you can achieve them.

So when you set a goal, think of all the actions you can take to achieve that goal. Better yet, write them down. The more you can come up with, the better.

When you start to consider the real details of achieving your goal, the goal itself becomes more real and reachable. Developing a list of specific actions, will enable you to see yourself doing it. As you begin to actually take those actions, your goal becomes more and more real to you.

Once you believe you can, you can. And that belief comes from a clear, specific set of actions that you can see yourself taking. Set your goal. In your mind, build a road to that goal. Then start walking down that road of success.

Stay in touch with your dreams

Another day dawns. Work to be done, problems to be solved, bills to be paid, disputes to settle. Mail to be answered, phone calls to make, errands to run.

Why? What is it all for? What does it all mean?

Nothing more or less that what you make of it. With no dream to follow, even the most "glamorous" life can be drudgery. Yet with a vision and a clear direction, even the most "mundane" life can be a thrill and a joy. It all depends on where you see yourself going.

Somewhere deep inside of you, you have a dream. You have

a vision of the world as you'd like it to be. You have a unique gift to offer. It may be covered up by years and years of the details of everyday life — but it's there. And when you look deeply enough, you'll find it. The person inside of you that wants to soar, to express, to create, to build, to love, to inspire, to live.

The chores and setbacks of everyday life can be a prison, or a pathway. It all depends on you. No matter how far "down" you think you are, there is always hope. There is always hope. There is always hope, for you are always capable of following your dream. You have a special gift. Deep inside, you know what it is. Find it and hold on to it. It will carry you through whatever you need to endure.

Move yourself to a new state

Your state of mind has a major influence on everything in your life. The results you achieve in any arena — work, family, sports, social — are due, for the most part, to your state of mind.

Your conscious mind can only hold one thought at a time. From moment to moment, you control what that thought is. So any time a negative thought works its way into your mind, you must replace it with a positive thought. The trick is to have that positive thought ready and waiting to use whenever you need it.

And the best way to do that is with clear, meaningful, precisely formulated goals for your life. They make for great positive thoughts that will quickly and effectively improve your state of mind.

When doubt, fear, anxiety or depression threaten to sidetrack you, focus on your goals. Imagine that you have already achieved them. Visualize yourself doing what you've always wanted to do. See yourself driving that new car, living in that house on the hill, sailing the ocean. Make the scene bright and clear in your mind, and play it over and over.

The Daily Motivator To Go

It takes a conscious effort, along with discipline and practice. And it will keep you continually focused and highly effective in everything you do.

What exactly do you want?

The way to get passionate about your goals, is to be clear and specific about them. Just saying that you want to "be rich and see the world" is much too vague. It doesn't conjure up any images to motivate you.

Say to yourself "I want to see the world." Does that do much for you? Now, try this: "I want to go hiking in the Himalayas, cruise along the coast of Alaska, walk along the beaches of St. Barts." See how much more passionate that feels.

When you are absolutely clear about what you want, you're halfway there. Anything that can be clearly defined, can be achieved. The time you take to determine exactly what you're after, and the time you spend visualizing the achievement of your goals, will pay enormous dividends.

See where you're going. See exactly where you're going, and you'll get there.

The stairway to your goal

Envision your goal at the top of a stairway and yourself at the bottom. Now look way up at the top, and see your goal. Then look at the next step down from the top. That would be the last step you need to take before you accomplish your goal. What is that step? And what is the step before it, and the one before that?

Identify the steps, all the way down to the very first one, the one that's right in front of you. That is the step you can take today. Stand up tall, focus on the top of the stairway, and take that first step. You're on your way! Now all you need to do is just keep taking those steps, one after one.

Don't waste your time waiting for the stairway to turn into an escalator that will carry you effortlessly to the top. It won't happen. You've got to take those steps yourself.

It will take some effort. The higher the goal, the more steps there will be. But as long as you're going to be walking up the stairway, you might as well have something great waiting at the top.

Take one step at a time, and you are certain to make it. You may occasionally slip, and you might want to sit and rest every now and then. The important thing, though, is to keep on climbing. Every moment, every day. Each step will carry you closer to the top.

And on that happy day when you take the last step, give yourself a little break. Relax for a moment, and look down the stairway at how far you've come. Squint your eyes and see if you can make out the people down there, the ones who are just now starting to climb.

Then take a deep breath, pat yourself on the back, and go look for the next stairway.

Micro-Goals

One of the best ways to experience success is to... experience success. By that, I mean that success in reaching your goals is largely a product of momentum.

If you can keep the momentum going long enough, you can reach any goal you set out to achieve. To build and maintain that momentum often requires a gradual process of setting and reaching higher and higher goals.

This is where the use of micro-goals can help. Micro-goals take the concept of "one day at a time" and break it down even further. Micro-goals will get you in the habit of setting goals, and in the habit of reaching them as well. This, in turn, will provide you with the experience of success on a regular and continuing basis.

What is a micro-goal? It is a small, easily achieved portion or fraction of a goal. Suppose your ultimate goal is to write a book. That is a daunting task, and one that cannot be easily achieved in an afternoon, a week, or even a month. So you break it into micro-goals. A micro-goal might be to write a paragraph in the next 5 minutes. Now that is something you can do immediately. Your success in reaching this micro-goal will come quickly, and the experience of that success will inspire you to set another goal. Perhaps a chapter by tomorrow afternoon. Or perhaps another 4 paragraphs in the next twenty minutes. These fractional goals are all helping you reach your ultimate goal. However, since they are quickly achieved, they prevent you from being overwhelmed, while at the same time providing you with very positive feedback.

The key to reaching your ultimate goal is to attach these micro-goals end to end in an upward spiral. Use micro-goals to get yourself in the habit of setting and reaching goals, and to move steadily in the direction you have chosen.

There's a reason

Our hopes and dreams are what make us great. They push us to do whatever it takes to reach them. They give us the enthusiasm with which we inspire others to see our vision. They help us through all the obstacles along the way.

There is a reason for the dreams that you have. Your dreams are yours so that you will follow them. The pain you feel if you're not following your dream, has the same purpose as any other pain — to get your attention and prompt you to correct the situation.

The joy you feel when pursuing your dream is there to keep you on the path.

The value of your dream is in the person you become by following it — in the skills you learn, in the people you help, in the growth you experience.

Dare to dream big dreams. The bigger your dream, the more motivation it will give you. When you put your dreams into action, you'll learn who you are. As you follow your dreams, you'll discover skills, passions, knowledge and desires that were meant for you. You'll find the essence that makes you unique.

Your dreams are not there to frustrate you, but to guide you toward the essential, joyful, abundant expression of creation that you are.

Don't let them steal your dream

Keep away from people who try
to belittle your ambitions. Small
people always do that, but the
really great make you feel that
you, too, can become great.
> — Mark Twain

The world is full of people who will be happy to tell you why your ideas will not work. People who will laugh at you for daring to dream big dreams. People who will call you crazy for pursuing your goals.

Just ignore them. Their pettiness and mean-spiritedness is their problem, not yours. Sadly, some people take delight in destructive criticism. Constructive, caring criticism is very useful and necessary. But criticism for its own sake is something to simply to be ignored.

Small minded people think that somehow they can improve their own lot by putting down others. Small minded people have a zero-sum mentality — they believe that people gain success only at the expense of others.

Nothing could be further from the truth.

True success comes only from providing something of value to the world. Your dreams, your ambitions do not diminish the lives of others. When you improve your own life, you cannot help but improve the lives of those around you.

What is life for, if not to reach for the stars?

Control and responsibility

Who's to blame?

Who is to blame for your troubles? The government, the economy, your boss, your customers, your spouse, your neighbors, your children, your parents, your employees, the mayor, big business?

When you blame others for your problems, you give them control over your life.

The only way to control your own life is to take responsibility for it. You are the reason for your own circumstances. You got yourself where you are today.

Is that depressing? Discouraging? No, of course not. Because the past is gone. It doesn't matter what has happened up to this point. The important thing is to take responsibility for your situation. Take responsibility, take action, and make your life what you want it to be. Blaming others for your problems might make you feel better about the past, but so what? What does it matter what you feel about the past?

What matters is this — what are you going to do today? Are you going to sit back and complain about how badly you've been treated? Or are you going to stand up and make a life of excellence for yourself? The choice is yours. You are responsible for your situation and your actions. You are in control. You can go wherever you desire to go, so you might as well make it someplace great.

Step up and take responsibility

The people who get what they want in life are those who are willing to take responsibility. Think about it — who would you rather deal with? Someone who makes excuses, and blames other people for everything that goes wrong, or someone who takes responsibility and gets the problem solved no matter whose "fault" it is?

When you are willing to take responsibility, you immediately stand out from the crowd. You become an effective, "can-do", results-oriented person. You're a leader and an achiever. It's only logical that when you're willing to accept more responsibility, you'll get more responsibility.

Take responsibility for your own work. For your own career. For your own surroundings. For your own health. Avoid blaming others for your problems, because that gives them control over your life. The moment you take responsibility, you become the master of your own destiny.

Take charge, take control, take responsibility.

Self reliance

Whatever is happening to you today, is a direct result of the things you did yesterday. If what you're doing is working, then keep on doing it! If what you're doing is not working, then change it. Don't just hope that things will get better. Do something about it. Take action. Take responsibility for your life. No one is going to do it for you.

Your life will change when you decide to change. When you learn new skills, meet new people, provide value to others. When you start each day with a clear purpose and direction. When you commit to doing whatever is necessary to reach your goals.

Life will throw obstacles in your path. You must decide whether to use each of those obstacles as an excuse for failure, or as a stepping stone to success. You can't control the cards you are dealt, but you can control how you play them. And therein lies the key to a life of accomplishment.

No matter how much money you have in the bank, or what kind of car is in your garage, or how many people have hurt you, or what you've done in the past, one thing is certain. The value in your own life comes directly from you.

Don't just wish for a better life — you can make it so!

Consequences

A life full of woe and a life full of joy are both the result of the same basic principle — that the quality of your life is determined by your actions. Everything you do has consequences. The things you do today will determine your life tomorrow.

You have hopes, and dreams, and desires. What are you doing right now that will make them happen? Right now is the time to act — it is the only time that is ever available to you. "Someday" will never come unless you take action today.

Everything has consequences. Whether that is good news or bad news is completely up to you.

You are in control

As you go through your day today, make a point to remember something. Keep this thought in mind at all times:

You are in control.

This is an empowering concept when you truly believe it. Just keeping this thought in mind allows you to change your life, and the lives of people around you.

Remember — you are in control. You are in control of all your actions. Remember that you're in control, and you'll be free to make the most of the time you have available to you. You are in control of your attitude. No one else can make you depressed, or lonely or excited. It is your reaction to others that determines your attitude. And that is something you can change instantly.

You are in control of your body. You can eat that chocolate doughnut or you can eat a banana instead. It is completely up to you. You can take a walk around the block or you can sit in front of the TV. No one can make you do either activity.

You are in control of your relationships. No one can make

you feel hurt unless you let them. No one can make you feel loved unless you react with love to their actions. If you want a better relationship with someone, then have a better relationship with them.

You're in control of your fears. If there is someone you've been putting off calling because it might embarrass you, then wait no longer. Only you can make yourself embarrassed.

You are in control of your time. You can choose to make the most of every single minute, or you can choose to waste a lot of time. It is your choice.

You are in control of your own mind. You decide what to think about things and how to react to different situations. You are in control of what your mind is thinking — whether it is thinking negative thoughts or positive thoughts, whether it is lamenting problems or looking for opportunities. It is up to you.

You are in control of your own consequences. Whatever happens to you happens because of you. This is a big step. Learning to accept consequences and responsibility will give you more power than you ever dreamed possible.

You are the sum of the choices you have made. You're in control anyway — you might as well use that control to create the person you want to be. If you're unhappy with any situation or person or other aspect of your life, take control and resolve the problem. It is your life, after all. No one else should live it for you. Life is made of choices, not chances. Make the choice to wisely exercise your control, today and every day.

Winners make it happen

Do you know anyone who always complains that they have to do things? "I *have* to go to work today. I *have* to finish that report. I *have* to pay the bills. I *have* to take my family to the park."

The winners in life realize that no one *has* to do anything. Everything you do, you do by choice. When you blame other people and situations for your troubles, you are giving them complete control over your life. Looking for someone to blame is the easiest way of avoiding responsibility. And if you continually avoid responsibility you'll succeed in completely losing control over your own life. If you feel you have to do a lot of things that you don't want to do, realize that you made the choices which put you in that position.

The good news is that you can also make the choices which will get you out of that position. It all starts with taking responsibility for your own life.

Instead of complaining that you have to do things, decide to do things. Set a direction for your life, and decide to do the things that will get you where you want to go. You can have control over your own life, if only you'll step up and take charge of it. Quit blaming and start acting responsible for your own fate.

Freedom of choice

There is no better measure
of a person than what he does
when he is absolutely free
— Wilma Askinas

We all have things we HAVE to do. What do you do because you WANT to do it? That is what defines you. When you've run out of things that need to be done, do you know what to do with yourself?

Life gives us what we ask of it. People who know what they want to do, generally spend much of their time doing it. And those who don't really know what they want, spend much of their time in the service of someone else's dream.

Freedom and responsibility go hand in hand. If you blame others for the circumstances of your life, you give them power over you. You can never be free as long as you make other people responsible for your life.

Only when you accept the responsibility of guiding your

own life, can you truly be free to live abundantly.

Choices, not chances, determine our destiny. Choose to spend your time on a life of excellence.

Mistakes

Do not look where you fell,
but where you slipped.
     — African proverb

If you're taking action, you'll make mistakes. When you make a mistake, that's great! You just learned something.

Admit your mistakes and examine them carefully. Take responsibility for them, and learn from them. Mistakes are superb teachers. Knowing what doesn't work, can be a tremendous help in determining what will work.

Tom Watson, the founder of IBM, well understood the value of mistakes. Once, one of his employees made a huge mistake that cost the company millions of dollars. The employee, upon being called into Watson's office, said "I suppose you want my resignation." "Are you kidding," replied Watson. "I just spent ten million dollars educating you."

Successful, effective people learn from everything that happens, including mistakes. When you make a mistake, the best policy is to pick up the pieces and look carefully at what happened. Don't tear yourself up over it. Just examine it and learn from it. Then apply your new knowledge and try again.

Time is what we make it

We must come to see that human progress never rolls in on
wheels of inevitability. It comes through the tireless efforts
and persistent work of men willing to be co-workers with God,
and without this hard work time itself becomes an ally of the
forces of social stagnation. — Martin Luther King, Jr.

Time does not cure all ills, time does not make things better. It is only through living, and striving, and struggling against the challenges, that things are made better.

Time is not our servant. Neither is it our oppressor. Time is our workplace, and our raw material. We can fashion it in any way we choose, through focus and effort.

And time comes to us in doses of now. Now is the only time we have, to do what we must do. If we wait until the "right" time, it never comes. Things will only be "right" when we act to make them so. Now is the only time we have, and now is when we must act.

We must expect the best — of ourselves, and of others. And then we must work to make it so.

Control yourself

He who conquers others is strong;
He who conquers himself is mighty.
                    — Lao-tzu

There is no need to control other people when you're able to control yourself. For some reason though, we all want to control others, and not ourselves. Why is this? Because we want to control, but we don't want to BE controlled (even by ourselves).

Well, it doesn't work that way. Someone is going to control you. It will either be your or someone else. If you spend your time and energy trying to control others, and neglect to control yourself, then someone will step in to fill the void. And the very attempt to control others gives them control over you.

What a waste of effort! Simply take control of your own self, of your own life. You are full of infinite possibilities. You are blessed with intelligence and energy. Take control. Your actions, purposely directed, will bring anything you desire.

Responsibility

The only way to control your own life is to take responsibility for it.

Yes, there are always circumstances to blame. Yes, there are those who would hold you back. Yes, there are things beyond your control.

Take responsibility anyway. People who achieve greatness, believe that whatever happens to them, they are responsible for it. It may seem unfair, yet it is ultimately liberating.

Whining will get you nowhere. Stepping up and taking responsibility, puts you in control. Take responsibility. Even if it's not your fault, it's your life. Even if it's not your assignment, it's your job.

You have a choice. You can always find someone, or something, to blame, and thereby allow circumstances and other people to control your life. Or, you can step up and take responsibility, no matter what. That puts you firmly in control, and gives you the power to live your life the way you choose.

Challenges

Life is difficult

I can think of nothing less pleasurable than a life devoted to pleasure.
— John D. Rockefeller, Jr.

Here's a little secret and a paradox. Once you truly accept the fact that life is difficult, it becomes vastly easier. When you stop fighting with life and accept it for what it is — the ultimate challenge — that acceptance gives you the perspective you need to overcome any obstacle. When you understand that life is a challenge, then you start to seek challenges, and those challenges build and shape a life of purpose and accomplishment.

We waste so much time trying to make life easy, when we could be spending our energy making life good. Turning obstacles into achievements is the very essence of life.

Joy comes not from comfort, but from living and contributing and achieving.

What would you want?

What if you could have any material thing, just by asking for it? What if you could just snap your fingers and anything, and everything, would just appear? A huge home on your own private island, the finest automobiles and aircraft, the most incredible gourmet food and fine wine, beautiful jewels and clothing. The best of everything.

What would you still want? What would you hunger for, day and night? What would be the one thing you could not have, if you could have anything you wished for?

Challenge.

Just think how empty life would be if you had no challenge. What would all the other things be worth, if they required no effort? Nothing.

The value of anything comes from what we put into it. Challenge is a wonderful gift, because it gives so much value, meaning and adventure to life.

Look for challenge. Welcome challenge. And delight in the challenges of life. They are what will make you the person you want to be.

Venturing out of the comfort zone

One of the biggest enemies of accomplishment is comfort. Most people are so attached to being comfortable, that they're just not willing to do what it takes to succeed. Meeting people, learning new skills, presenting your ideas, taking risks, working hard — these are all very uncomfortable, and all very necessary for success.

You must decide whether you want a life of comfort or a life of accomplishment. You can have anything, do anything, and be anything you want, if you'll just step outside your comfort zone and take the actions that need to be taken.

Look at the things you do each day and ask yourself why you're doing them. Is it because they're familiar, and comfortable, and secure? Are you anxious about venturing outside of your cozy comfort zone? Are there things you avoid doing because they might cause you some discomfort?

Accomplishment requires that you step outside of your comfort zone. The good news is that when you venture beyond the borders, your comfort zone expands. Success in one area of your life will give you more confidence in everything you do.

Don't let yourself get too comfortable. A short time of discomfort is far better than a lifetime of regret.

Confront it

Everything we avoid, or deny, or try to run away from, can serve to defeat us in the end. And anything, no matter how much we despise it or how unpleasant it is, can be turned into

72   *The Daily Motivator To Go*

a source of growth and power, when openly confronted.

Problems will not just go away if they are ignored. Failing to confront something negative, serves only to give more power and influence to it. And when you finally are forced to deal with it, it has grown to be quite nasty. Yet when you confront your problems, you grow as a person, and gain true power over your life.

We know we should confront life, yet fear holds us back. And we take it to another level when we try to deny our problems — we actually fear the fear, so we try not to even admit it exists.

The only way around this is to feel the fear and do it anyway. Deal with the things that must be dealt with. Confront life head on. Nothing is gained by living in fear. Decide to play an active role in your life.

Is it uncomfortable? Yes. Is it difficult? Yes. What will everyone else think? Who cares! Your life, your goals, your dreams are worth the pain and the effort. Stop hiding behind your fears. Once you start to take action, once you make the commitment to do whatever it takes, the strength and the resources you need will come to you. Begin today to confront the obstacles in your life, and let your own unique light shine brightly.

Feel the burn

In body building and other athletic training, there's a saying, "No pain — no gain." If you're going to work out, you've got to be prepared to "feel the burn" in your muscles. The challenge of running, cycling, rowing, skiing, swimming, lifting weights or any other exercise, is what builds strong, healthy bodies.

Challenge can help to build a strong, healthy mind and spirit as well. Like strenuous physical exercise, challenges of all kinds are uncomfortable.

Challenges demand new thinking. They demand hard work and sacrifice. And every challenge helps you to grow.

Life itself is a challenge. Just the fact that you've survived this long means you're pretty good already at meeting challenges. And the better you become at accepting and confronting challenge, the better your life will be.

May you be blessed with many problems

Be grateful for your problems. You are more committed, more focused, more effective when you have no choice but to be. You're more likely to prevail when you MUST prevail.

Great achievements don't usually happen just because someone thought it would be a fun thing to do in their spare time. Great achievements come about because they must, because there is no other choice.

Which are you more likely to regret — time wasted in idleness, or time spent overcoming the obstacles in your way?

The obstacles teach us. The problems force us to grow, to live, to appreciate what we have and to know who we are. They are a blessing. When we have no other choice, we can do amazing things.

Why do children climb up slides?

If you've ever spent much time at a playground you've seen that small children love to slide down slides, and that they also love to climb up them. Playground slides are not designed to climb. They are steep and slippery, and have no hand holds. And that is precisely the attraction for little ones — the challenge.

We're all born with the desire to seek out and overcome challenges. For the better part of human history, it's what has kept people alive. And it has led to a steadily continuing increase in our standard of living.

Challenges can teach, inspire and help us to grow. And overcoming challenge brings a sense of accomplishment and the confidence to face even greater challenges.

Sometimes, though, we get so caught up in security and

comfort, that we're reluctant to take on challenges. But such complacency is at best boring, and over time can erode the essence of life.

Challenges are a key part of childhood. Children learn to overcome obstacles on a daily basis to be able to walk, communicate, eat and socialize. In fact, you could say that challenge is the essence of youth. If you think of yourself as "old" then you're probably not experiencing enough challenge. And if you want to always stay young, never stop seeking new challenges.

Rejoice in the challenges

If you feel like giving up, your dream isn't big enough.

Whenever you attempt anything, you will have challenges. There will be days when you wonder if anything will ever come of your efforts. People will scoff at you, laugh at you, conspire against you, and ignore you. Deals will fall through, things will break, people will lie to your face.

Remember that the challenges are not there to stop you. The challenges are there to help you grow. To help you be the person who can attain the dream you're following. In fact, the person you become in the pursuit of your dream is worth far more than any dream could ever be.

Be thankful for the hard times, for the challenges. Because what they give you, no one can ever take away.

Push yourself

If you want to know the satisfaction of accomplishment, then you must also feel the apprehension that comes from pushing yourself to the edge of your abilities. In order to grow, we must venture out into unknown territory. We must take on challenges that make us uncomfortable.

It can be frightening, taking on new challenges. And we are so fearful of fear, eager to avoid fearful situations.

Have you ever considered, though, the benefits of fear? Fear gives us a heightened sense of alertness and razor sharp focus. We breathe a little deeper to take in more oxygen, and the heart beats a little faster. Fear blocks out all the trivial stuff, and gives us increased energy. Isn't that exactly what we need to take on a difficult challenge? Is fear really so bad?

Venture out. Reach higher than what you're comfortable with. Push yourself to the point where you feel the exciting apprehension that gives you the motivation and the energy to win.

Not so easy

Value is created by effort. It requires commitment, and sacrifice, and action — lots of action, over and over again.

So why do so many people look for an easy way out?

Somehow we have gotten the idea that life should be easy. That's a lie. It's a seductive message at first blush, yet when you think about it, would you really want life to be easy?

The only people who have it "easy" are buried six feet under the ground. If you are alive, things are not easy. By its very definition, life is not easy. Life is composed of activity, challenge and struggle. Give up the illusion that life can ever be easy. You wouldn't want it to be.

Instead, let your life be grand, glorious, challenging and full of accomplishment. That beats easy any day!

Stop wasting your time looking for an easy way out, and get on with the exciting business of meeting the challenges of life. That is where you'll find joy and fulfillment.

The Daily Motivator To Go

Discipline and focus

The power of discipline

Discipline gives us the means to enjoy life. Some would say that discipline is limiting, that the spirit should be free from any kind of rules or limits so as to foster creativity. But creativity without focus, without skills, is wasted. Without a disciplined understanding of light and perspective, the artist cannot express herself. Without disciplined study of language and culture, the writer cannot adequately convey his insight. Without disciplined knowledge of chords and rhythms, the musician cannot express his creativity.

Discipline gives life a context. It is not confining, but rather is enabling. Without discipline there is confusion. Yes, your spirit can soar without discipline, but it cannot stay aloft for very long that way. Discipline is the foundation for accomplishment.

Discipline is not ever the easiest option. It is a full time activity. You can't just be disciplined in one area of your life — true discipline must be consistent.

Remember that for every disciplined effort, there are multiple rewards. A life of discipline leads to a constant upward spiral of achievement. Look around your life, see what needs to be done, and do it now. That's discipline.

Getting in the habit

It is just as easy to get into a "good" habit as it is to get into a "bad" habit. That's a little secret that successful people live by. In fact it is really just as easy to be successful as it is to be unsuccessful. It is just a matter of choice. You can spend your time doing the things that will bring you closer to your goals, or you can spend your time seeking immediate comfort and gratification.

People complain that "it's too hard to exercise every day." That's nonsense. Exercise and movement are joyful, natural conditions that make us feel great. It's not hard. It's just that they're in the habit of not exercising. Once they make the choice to exercise, it is no more difficult than sitting on the couch watching TV.

Success in anything can be summed up very concisely. It's really quite simple. First, know what you want and know the reasons you want it. Second, determine exactly what you need to do to get it. Third, make a habit of doing those things that you need to do. That's really all there is to it. It's not complicated, and it is within the reach of anyone.

Oh, yes, you may think you need to have the right amount of self esteem, or the proper training, or the ideal environment, or support from your family, or any number of things. While all these things are fine, they're not necessary. All that's needed is the desire, the plan, and the action. If your desire is strong enough, you'll find a way to get the things you need. If your plan is well-constructed, it will take you where you want to go, as long as you have the discipline to follow through on it.

Life is the result of choices. You are where you are because of the choices you have made in the past. Your future depends on the choices you make today. You can choose to have that extra beer, or you can choose to read another chapter in a good book. You can choose to act on an opportunity, or you can choose to sleep late. All these choices add up to your situation in life. And if you get in the habit of making the right choices, the choices that move you closer to your goals, then you'll fulfill the enormous potential that is inside of you.

Indulgence

One of the best ways to become disciplined is to indulge yourself on a regular basis. At first that might sound contradictory. When you think about it, though, indulgence can be a key tool in developing and maintaining discipline.

Discipline always requires denial. For example, if you want to discipline yourself to lose weight, you must deny yourself fattening foods. When you discipline yourself to work hard toward achieving goals you've set for yourself, you deny yourself some of the "fun" activities of life.

We're only human, though, and we need incentives along the way. One powerful incentive is to keep yourself focused on your goals, on the objects of your discipline. Another good way is to schedule a regular indulgence. It's better if your indulgence is something you do regularly — every day, every week. It is important to be able to look forward to it. And when the time comes, enjoy it. Savor every minute without the least bit of guilt. Take time for yourself and reward yourself for your hard work and discipline. And remember that you'll get the opportunity again, so there's no need to "binge." (I use "binge" here in a generic sense, not just as it applies to food.)

One powerful way to take this concept to a higher level is to develop indulgences that actually enhance your discipline. A good example of this is physical exercise. If you can find an exercise that it also a true indulgence, then you can discipline and indulge at the same time. That is a powerful combination.

Try a little indulgence — you deserve it and it will help to keep you on track.

Planting Seeds

Farmers can cause an abundance of food to literally spring out of the ground. First, however, they must plant the seeds.

Our society has become accustomed to instant gratification. Television brings us instant entertainment, delivery services move our stuff overnight, the Internet gives us instant mail, the telephone gives us instant conferences, pagers let us find people instantly, microwave ovens and fast food restaurants provide instant food. The list goes on and on.

The quickening pace of life increasingly hides one important truth: that some of the best things in life take time. Things like relationships, experience, education, skills and wealth. When you expect to get these things overnight, you end up spinning your wheels.

You must learn to plant seeds, and then nurture them while they take root and grow. How do you know what seeds to plant? That's where your long-term goals come in to play. To get where you want to be a couple of years from now, it's important to start laying the groundwork today.

Live your life today, enjoying all the excitement of this fast-paced world. And remember to plan for tomorrow, planting seeds along the way.

Working harder makes work easier

What? That seems like a contradiction. It's not.

Do the hard work first. Go ahead and get it out of the way in the beginning. When you do that, it makes everything that comes after it much easier. For one thing, if you do the hard work first, you don't have it "hanging over your head" all the time. You don't have to spend time and effort worrying about it because it's already done!

Even more importantly, doing the hard work first almost always gives you a solid foundation and preparation that makes everything else flow much more smoothly. When you work hard now, you'll work less later. And you'll be more effective, too.

Generally, the hardest part of any project is also the most critical. When you do the hard part first, you're less likely to run into a time crunch at the end. After all, when the critical part is already done, the other stuff can slip if it has to.

You're going to have to do the hard part sooner or later. So you might as well do it sooner, get it over with, and start reaping the benefits from it right away.

Over the wall

Endurance athletes refer to it as "the wall." It's that agonizing period, fairly early in the race, when the body just doesn't want to keep going. Experienced competitors know that once they get through "the wall", things get much easier and they can just keep going and going. In fact, the next milestone is referred to as "runner's high" — an absolute euphoria that lies on the other side of "the wall."

The same profile usually occurs in any effort, whether in business, relationships, or other kinds of projects. It's easy to get started on something. You have plenty of excitement and adrenaline. Once you're up and running, you begin to approach the wall. That's where the vast majority of people give up. That's where you are met head-on by the difficult challenges. It is what separates winners from all the rest. It is NOT the time to give up.

Muster all your strength and your will, and make yourself get through the wall. Meet the difficult challenges early on, and keep forging ahead. You'll soon be over the wall. Then the going will get smooth, and your progress will be swift, even to the point of euphoria.

It sure beats, quitting, and having to start all over again.

Focus

Every day, you're making an investment of something extremely valuable — your time. You cannot save time for use later. It must be used as it comes. We all get the same amount of it — 24 hours each day. Success is determined largely by how effectively we use our time.

Get the most out of the time you have. Focus your efforts on doing the things that will have the most significant impact on your life and your work. Do the "big" things first, and stay "on task" until they're done.

Nothing will make you more effective than the ability to stay focused. Practice it. Work at it. Challenge yourself to stay in focus. When you're about to become distracted, force yourself back to the task at hand. You'll be amazed at how much more you get done, when you actually work the whole time you're working.

Your time is precious and cannot be replaced once it is spent. Use it wisely and effectively, by staying focused and getting things done.

Bit by bit

You can have, do, or be whatever you want if you will commit to it consistently. That means doing something every day, every hour, or even every minute, over and over again until your goal is realized.

Little things, done again and again, have enormous power. Picking up the phone and calling prospects, practicing a musical instrument, writing chapter after chapter in a book. Success comes from the consistent application of effort.

The reason that most people are living mediocre lives is that they're just not disciplined to do work consistently. It's easier to take a 2-hour lunch, or skip class, or just find a job where someone else tells you exactly what to do. Initiative and consistent effort require constant commitment.

Imagine that you're leaving for lunch in seven minutes. That's plenty of time to make another phone call. On the other end of that call may be your future best customer. It's easy to rationalize that you don't have enough time to make another call. It's easy to find "busy work" to do for seven minutes — looking though your mail again, backing up the files on your computer, tidying up your desk, programming your friend's number into your phone. It's easy to let that seven minutes get away from you.

But just killing time won't get you anywhere. Sure it's a little painful to make a few extra calls, to practice a little longer, to work a few more minutes on your proposal. But which pain would you rather have: the small pain of discipline or the enormous pain of regret when you lose the big sale and have to explain to your kids why you can't take them to Disney World?

Get in the habit of doing the little things over and over again. You'll leave the competition in the dust and create a life of excellence.

Vigilance

It is difficult for many people to keep weight off, but it is far easier to keep weight off than it is to lose weight. It's a bit of trouble to get the oil changed in your car, but it's easier than replacing your engine. Painting your house is difficult, but it is much easier to paint wood than it is to replace it if, unpainted, it rots. It is easier for a nation to prevent a war by strength than to fight a war that someone else starts.

Unfortunately, in our desire for new success, we often fail to maintain the things we already have. But in the end, keeping a constant vigilance pays off. When you put some time and effort into maintaining the good things in your life, then you are far better prepared to take advantage of the opportunities that come your way. Rust and rot are always waiting if you're not constantly on guard. Don't let them steal your life.

Life is less costly when you pay as you go. Don't neglect what you already have — you may need it someday. Your physical possessions, your health, your relationships, your skills, your knowledge — all these need regular attention lest you lose them to decay.

It may not be as exciting as seeking new accomplishments, but vigilance is just as important to a successful life. Maintain your ship so you'll be ready to sail when the wind is fair and there's a treasure to be had.

Preparation

There is no shortage of opportunity. Every day presents every person with countless opportunities to be, or do, or create whatever is desired.

Yet few people ever take advantage of the opportunities that come their way. Not because they don't want to, but because they're unable to. Because they are not adequately prepared.

We often look at highly successful people, and conclude that their success is the result of being "in the right place at the right time." While that is true, it was not random good fortune that put them there. It was preparation that helped them to see the opportunity in the first place, and then to make the most of that opportunity.

Preparation is not usually fun or exciting. It can be tedious and unfulfilling in the short term. Yet it is absolutely essential. To enjoy success, you must discipline yourself, day after day, to develop your skills, increase your knowledge, make new personal contacts, and lay the groundwork for your success.

When you prepare yourself, you're always in the right place at the right time.

Rise above your burdens

The most senseless burdens are those of our own making. We live for the moment, and disregard the future consequences. We eat too much, exercise too little, put all sorts of chemicals into our bodies. We let things slip, we fail to follow up. We take shortcuts. It all adds up and brings us down.

Yet, what you get yourself into, you have the power to get out of. There is always hope. The same passion and energy that got you into the mess can get you out. It all depends on your focus. Is it on the next cigarette, or the next century?

Life can be so much more. Taking the easy way out, is no way to live. The effort, the commitment, the discipline — they are their own rewards. You cannot consume a great life, you must create it. There is no easy way out, because the effort IS the fulfillment.

Right this moment, you can rise above your self-imposed burdens, just by deciding to do so, and by making the commitment to make a difference, in your own life and the lives of others. Put out the effort, every minute of every day. Life is worth it.

Think for yourself

Thinking is hard work, which is probably why so few people ever attempt it. It is much easier to simply react, to accept someone else's vision, to go along with "conventional wisdom", to keep making the same mistakes over and over again.

A successful life demands some thinking. That means carefully considering options, projecting your actions into the future, applying proven concepts to your own unique situation, creating strategies. This may sound like heavy stuff, yet you don't need a fancy graduate degree to do it. All you need is some reasonable, common sense. That, and the willingness to tackle the job of thinking for yourself.

As you go through your day, notice how much, or how little, you actually think about what you're doing. What percentage of your actions are on "autopilot"? How much do you do because that's the way you've always done it?

Make it a point to stop and think every once in a while. Think about why you do the things you do, where your actions are leading you, what you could do to be more effective. The reluctance to think is a trap. It forces you to work in the service of someone else's dream, and to settle for less than you're capable of achieving.

The desire for easy answers enslaves too many people to lives of mediocrity. The way out of the trap is to think for yourself. Have the courage to ask the hard questions, and work to find the answers. Make a commitment every day to do the mental work that will lead to growth and achievement. Put some thought into your life, and you'll rise high above the crowd.

Are you in the habit of success?

Many of the things we do each day, we do by habit. Habits can be very useful. If we had to constantly think about everything we did, we wouldn't accomplish much. Habits can be a hindrance, too. They can weigh us down and hold us back.

The key to success is to develop habits that take you where you want to go. When you think about it, doing the right thing is not usually any more difficult than doing the wrong thing. It's just that we get ourselves in the wrong habits, and those habits hold us back.

For example, taking a walk every evening is a very pleasant, enjoyable, stimulating experience. While you're walking, you feel great. If gives you a lift. And it is very healthy for you.

So why do you stay home and watch the television every night instead of taking a pleasant walk? The answer — habit. Why do you reach for a bag of potato chips instead of an apple? Habit. The apple is just as tasty, and much healthier for you. But if you're in the habit of eating chips, that's what you'll eat.

Success in life takes effort, but it's not difficult or complicated. It is just a matter of knowing what you want, determining how to get it, and making a habit of doing those things that you need to do. Habits are very powerful, because they're actions that are repeated over and over again. The good ones are well worth the effort it takes to establish them.

Get in the habit of success. Choose your habits carefully, and they'll serve you well.

What's your pleasure?

Pleasure is a matter of conditioning. A teenager smoking her first cigarette doesn't enjoy it at all. She's almost certainly doing it to "fit in" and it probably even makes her a little sick. After a while, though, she likes it so much she finds it hard to quit.

"If it feels good, do it" was a popular rallying cry during the sex/drug revolution of the 60s and 70s. But what feels good? It depends. Certain people who consider themselves to have refined taste enjoy eating snails and fish eggs, while others are disgusted by the thought of eating such food.

By nature, we want to do what is pleasurable to us. And so pleasure is a powerful motivator. Add this to the fact that pleasures can be learned, and you have a potent strategy for achieving your success: Choose the pleasures that move you toward your goals.

For example, there is just as much potential for pleasure in jogging 2 miles as there is in eating a bag of potato chips. The person who is trying to get in top physical shape would be well advised to find his pleasure in the jogging rather than the chips.

Rather than finding ways to serve your pleasures, find pleasures that will serve you. Instead of taking pleasure in getting drunk, sitting in front of the TV, and complaining about other people, learn to find pleasure in walking around the neighborhood, discovering new ideas, finding new and better ways to do your job.

Just like everything else in your world, your pleasures are under your control. Use them to your advantage.

Choose your life

What is the difference between a life of joy and accomplishment, and a life of despair? What is the difference between a day spent effectively, and a day of idleness? What is the difference between positive direction and certainty, and just drifting along?

The difference comes from making choices. Look around you. The things that make up your world are the result of choices. The house where you live, your job, the size of your bank account, your family, the car you drive, the books on your shelf. All choices.

You can choose the life you want. Not in one single momentous choice, but in the little choices you make every day. Each day you choose when to wake up, what to eat, how much work you do, how much money you spend or save, how you talk to your children, how willing you are to learn. These are the choices that determine your life, and you make them every day.

Everything you do is a choice — an opportunity, that you cannot escape, to build your life. What that life becomes is entirely up to you.

Value and values

Think Value

When everyone else is looking for ways to TAKE, you can stand head and shoulders above the crowd by looking for ways to GIVE.

When you create value, you are always be in demand. In every situation, look for the possibilities. Don't worry about who thought of what, or who is to blame. Leave those petty concerns to those who are foolish enough to think they're important.

Think value. Think possibilities. What positive contribution can you make, that will make a difference? There is opportunity in every circumstance, when you have the will to do what needs to be done. The value you create speaks louder, longer and more positively about you than most anything else you could do or say.

Ask yourself this question

Who stands to gain more from your success than you do?

Wow. There's a world of power in that simply phrased question. It drives home the point that your success depends entirely on your ability to provide service and value to others. And it goes beyond that. Because not only can your customers gain from your success, but so can your suppliers, and so can other people with whom you may not even have a relationship.

For example, if you're selling residential real estate, your success could also mean success for a mortgage banker. Or a moving company. Or an interior designer. If you're selling computer hardware, your success can help people who sell computer software.

In the corporate world, there's a hot trend called strategic alliances. Computer companies form an alliance to develop and promote a technical standard. Disney and Burger King form an alliance take advantage of the popularity of "Toy Story." These strategic alliances are nothing more than an answer to the above question.

If you can find someone who stands to gain more from your success than you, then do you think you could enlist the support of that person? Of course! It's a no-brainer. How hard can it be to get someone to act in their own interest?

Ask yourself this question and be creative about your answer. You'll find a whole world of possibilities opening up.

Integrity

To thine own self be true.
And it must follow as the night the day,
thou canst not then be false
to any man. — Shakespeare

People love, value and honor a person of integrity. Integrity will bring true peace of mind to one's life, along with a quality and richness of living. A life of integrity is a life that is full of accomplishment and meaning.

In any situation, we have several choices. We can choose to do the easiest thing, or choose to do "what everybody else does", or we can choose to do the right thing. Integrity means doing the right thing every time.

Integrity is a passionate commitment to the truth, in what we do, what we say, and in our relationships with others. When we are true to ourselves, we cannot be false to anyone else.

Integrity means acting to make the world as much better as you possibly can. It means discovering your own unique set of skills and abilities, and using them to achieve maximum benefit for those around you. It means finding what you do best, and doing it with all the commitment and energy you can muster. There is no better path to success and accomplishment than this.

Providing value to others

What is work? For some people, work is hitting a golf ball. For others, that is considered play. For some people, work is flying an airplane. For others, flying is play. For some people, work is writing. For others, writing is considered a hobby.

The difference between work and recreation is not in the activity itself. The difference is in who benefits from the activity. When you are working, the assumption is that you're being compensated in some fashion for your activity. And that compensation comes from the value that you create for other people.

Work is wealth creation, and it can take many forms. We used to think of work as pure physical toil. That is an outdated perception. In fact, as machines take over much of the routine, repetitive work, the work of humans must become more creative in nature. It used to be that the majority of society or an enterprise would toil at physical tasks, and only an elite few would be free to think, create and innovate.

Now, however, it is incumbent upon just about everyone to be creative and innovative in their work. This is the concept of empowerment, and it is being used in the most successful of organizations. When people are empowered with more responsibility, they produce more value.

This works on any level. The formula is simple. If you want to create wealth, you must find a way to provide value to others. There are no limitations on what this can be. The more value you provide, and the more people you provide it to, the more wealth you will create.

The essence of value

Recently, I heard a young boy make the comment that "If I were President, I'd give everybody enough money to buy whatever they want."

As wonderful as this might sound at first blush, such a policy would be a complete disaster. If everyone could receive all the money they needed, without working, then there would be nothing to buy with that money. No one would work to produce the goods and services. Money would be meaningless.

The value of money, or of anything else, depends on the effort that must be expended to get it. A diamond and a pebble are both rocks, but diamonds are much more valuable because they are so hard to find. If diamonds were as plentiful as common pebbles, they would be virtually worthless.

There simply are no shortcuts. It is the effort needed to acquire a diamond that makes it so valuable. It is the work necessary to acquire it that gives money its value.

Life itself is that way, too. It is only worth what you put into it. A life of value and fulfillment is possible only you are willing to put forth an effort and give of yourself.

Don't cheat yourself out of life by trying to get "something for nothing." Your life is worth exactly what you put into it.

Do the right thing

For what will a man be profited, if he gains
the whole world, and forfeits his soul?
— Matthew 16:26

The quality of your life is ultimately determined by the integrity of your actions.

It may seem that doing what is right would sometimes call for a sacrifice on your part, would sometimes demand that you act against your own interest. Indeed, there are sacrifices to be made. However, you never sacrifice your own interest, when you do what is right. It is always the better choice for you, to do the right thing.

It is always in your best interest to live a life of integrity.

There are no shortcuts in life. You receive value, by being a valuable person. The abundance you enjoy is the abundance you create. It is a law that needs no enforcement, because it cannot be broken. When you take advantage of others, you

The Daily Motivator To Go

cheat yourself of the opportunity to provide real value, the opportunity to make a difference. What gain could possibly equal that loss?

What is truly important to you? The pleasure, the comfort, the expediency of the moment, or the meaning and value in your life? A life of quality is possible only with integrity, only when you remain constantly true to your highest ideals.

Something for nothing

If you expect something for nothing, then you need to raise your expectations. Because the only something you'll get for nothing is... nothing. And that's not much.

When you expect something for nothing, what do you really expect? Do you really expect you'll receive the best that life has to offer in return for contributing nothing? Do you think that somehow the universe should tilt in your favor, and that you should be able to take without giving back?

Let's imagine a "value expectation continuum." On the far left is "something for nothing." In the middle is "something for something". And on the far right is "nothing for something." So, the more you move to the right, the more you give, and the less you expect to receive in return. Guess where all the world's wealthiest, happiest, most fulfilled people are? They're way off to the right end of the spectrum. They create for the sake of creation.

Why? They've discovered that giving is infinitely more rewarding than taking. Not just in the context of morality, but also in dollars and cents. They give value, and that value is returned to them many times over.

Don't waste your time chasing "something for nothing." You wouldn't want it even if you got it.

Just imagine...

The value in your own life must come from you. You cannot take it from someone else, or borrow it, or inherit it, or marry it, or just get lucky and happen upon it. You must produce it.

Your life has meaning only to the extent that you make something of it. Only to the extent that you make your own unique contribution to the world.

Imagine that you are the most powerful and creative entity in the universe. That you have the power to create your own reality. And you have done so. You have created everything you ever could have imagined or hoped for. And yet you are bored by it all. You realize that your fulfillment comes through challenge, and there are no challenges left. So, being the limitless creative force that you are, you decide to create the ultimate challenge for yourself.

You put all your creative energy into building this ultimate challenge, excited by the prospect of being truly "alive" again. When it is all ready to go, you open the door that leads to your challenge, step inside...

And find yourself exactly as the person you are right now, in precisely the same situation that you are in today.

Now, how will you live out the adventure that you've worked so hard to create for yourself?

Kindness

When you give your kindness to someone, it's not gone — it's invested. We all need each other. No one can be successful by himself or herself. Sincere kindness builds relationships that enrich your life. Kindness and success go hand in hand.

We've all heard about the tough, no-nonsense business person who is highly successful in spite of their blatant disregard for everyone. Yes, that happens, but it is a rare exception. And though that person may have a degree of success in business, there's much more to life than that.

Trying to succeed in life without kindness is like running a race with your feet tied together. It can be done, but it puts you at a major disadvantage right from the start, and who would want to do it anyway?

Kindness doesn't mean that you should let people take advantage of you. Kindness doesn't mean that you should be indulgent or permissive. In fact, many times the kindest thing you can do is to be firm with someone, out of concern for their well being. As in "Friends don't let friends drive drunk." Kindness is strength and confidence.

The kindness and respect you give will come back to you, greatly multiplied. The best thing you can do for yourself, is to show true, sincere kindness toward others.

Shortcuts

Have you ever seen a car stuck in the grassy median of the freeway? Usually this was someone who wanted to turn around, but was in too much of a hurry to go all the way to the next exit. So he decided to take a "shortcut" through the middle, and got stuck in the mud or the ditch. Then, instead of spending an extra 5 minutes to go to the next exit and turn around, he must spend a few hours getting a tow truck to pull the car out.

Think about that the next time you're tempted to take a shortcut in your work, your relationships, your health, or anywhere else. The quick and easy way out often has a tremendous downside.

The value you get from life is equal to the effort you put in. In the end, searching for shortcuts usually takes more time and energy than just doing the work in the first place.

You simply cannot get something for nothing. Because whatever you get for nothing, regardless of its "market value", means nothing to you.

Everything comes back

It is impossible for the energy you put out not to come back to you eventually. It may take a while, and it may not come back to you in the way that you had expected, but it will come back.

You cannot turn on a light and remain in the darkness. Each and every effort you put forth will make the world around you brighter. And the more value you can add to the lives of others, the more your efforts will be multiplied.

Give to the world and the world will give back to you, many times over.

Reaching your dreams is not a matter of wishing, or taking. It requires action. You must build, and create, and participate. Give of yourself, because the reward is in the journey. Your dreams would be meaningless if they required no effort or energy.

By doing and by giving, you express the unique person that you are. And that is the essence of life.

Make a difference

Provide something of value to someone, and you have a job. Provide something of value to people, over and over again, and you have a profession. Provide something of great value to a large number of people and you have a fortune.

Life is not about taking. You can only take what's already there. Life is about giving and creating value. About making a difference. If you try to shortcut the process, it is you who will come up short in the end. When you take something you don't deserve, you might get it but you won't own it — it will own you.

Look for ways to make a difference in the world. To solve problems, to create joy and beauty, to give comfort, to provide meaning to the lives of others. Look for ways to give, look for things that need to be done. That is where you'll find opportunity. The more value you provide, and the more people you provide it to, the wealthier you will become — both materially and spiritually.

The bigger difference you make in the lives of others, the bigger results you'll see in your own life.

Gratitude

Gratitude

True abundance begins with gratitude and thankfulness. Being thankful focuses our attention on the things we do have, and helps those things to grow.

Make it a habit to tell people thank you. To express your appreciation, sincerely and without the expectation of anything in return. Truly appreciate those around you, and you'll soon find many others around you. Truly appreciate life, and you'll find that you have more of it.

The things you appreciate will grow — your customers, your business, your skills, your family, your faith, your self.

Do you want to "have it all"? With an attitude of gratitude you'll realize that you already do have it all. Everything you could ever desire is already inside of you. You simply need to appreciate it, and love it and nurture it enough so that it is fully expressed in your life.

Be thankful for the person you are, for the situation you're in, for the challenges you're given. That is the first step toward a positive, fulfilling life. Your sincere gratitude will bring you abundance.

Being thankful and appreciative

Taking the time to express appreciation is one of the most positive things you can do. It's a big boost for the other person — people love to know that they're appreciated. It's a great feeling for you, too.

And there's no better way to encourage people to do their best, than to let them know you appreciate what they're doing.

Beyond showing appreciation for other people, it's important to cultivate a general attitude of thankfulness. Stop and think about all the good things in your life and be thankful for them. Too often we focus on our problems and shortcomings, and that only gives them that much more control over our lives. Being thankful for the positive things in our lives helps us to focus on possibilities for improvement.

Think of someone to whom you've never before expressed appreciation and make it a point to let them know you're thankful for what they're doing. Make a habit of being thankful and appreciative for the positive things in your life. When you nurture and encourage the good things instead of dwelling on the problems, your life will be full of joy.

I'll be happy when...

When you define your happiness by what you don't have, then you can never be happy. If you feel you need more in order to be complete, then when you get it you'll still feel like you're lacking. We've all heard people say, "If only I had ____, then I'd be really happy." But happiness is what you are, not what you have.

Instead of focusing on what you don't have, be thankful for what you do have. Be actively thankful. Think about the fact that you are alive and be thankful for the air you breathe, the water you drink, the food you eat, the warmth of the sun, the coolness of an evening breeze. Be thankful for your family, your friends, the people who listen to you and care about you, the people who depend on you. Be thankful for your mind, and for your ability to use it to create things and solve problems, and for the education you have.

When you focus on the abundance that you already have, it will expand and grow.

Appreciate before you accumulate

You cannot ever have what you want, unless you learn to want what you have. When you're thankful and appreciative for the things you have, you begin to live abundantly.

The Daily Motivator To Go

Life isn't about getting, it is about being. Nothing you get will make you happy. Happiness comes from you. Only you can make yourself happy.

When you constantly focus on getting more, then you are acknowledging and fostering a mindset of lack and limitation. By contrast, appreciating what you have will keep you focused on abundance, and that will bring you all the good things you truly desire.

There's nothing wrong with ambition, but it won't get you anywhere unless it has a context and a purpose. Being frustrated and resentful about the things you don't have, won't get you very far. Enjoying every moment, without qualification, will give you the positive focus you need to achieve your goals.

Appreciate what you have by nurturing and building on it. Take good care of your body, your home, your family, your relationships, your environment, your skills, your mind, your values, of life itself.

Like a doting relative, life will give you more when you show appreciation for what you've already received.

What is RIGHT with your life?

Too often, we define our lives by what's wrong with us. That limits us, and keeps us negatively focused.

Stop for a moment and consider all the things that are right with your life. Look for the positive things and be sincerely thankful for them.

Gratitude is the cornerstone of abundance. When someone gives you a gift, and you neglect to thank them for it, will they ever give you another? It's not likely. Life is the same way. In order to attract more of the blessings that life has to offer, you must truly appreciate what you already have.

You have, within yourself, all the wealth and abundance that you'll ever need. All you have to do is recognize it and put it to use. And that starts with focusing on the positive.

What do you enjoy about life? When are you the happiest? What do you do better than anyone else you know? What gives you a sense of satisfaction? What is your passion? What would you do if your resources were unlimited?

Answer these questions, and you'll find the things that are right with your life. Get in touch with them and appreciate them. Find a way to make them a part of your daily life and your work. Help them to grow, and they will bring you fulfillment.

Appreciate your everything

Appreciate and value the time you have, and make the most of it. The richest, most successful person in the world, and the poorest person each have the same 24 hours in every day. The difference is in what they do with that time.

Appreciate and value your body — after all, it's where you're living. Fuel it with food that's rich in nutrition. Don't dump junk and poison into it. Keep it strong with regular exercise.

Appreciate and value your mind. Everything you accomplish, everything you become, must first exist in your mind. Constantly feed your mind with new ideas, new perspectives, new knowledge. Keep it strong with regular challenges.

Appreciate and value your skills and accomplishments, the people you know, your hobbies and interests, your passions, your opinions. These are the things that permit you to create value and make your own unique contribution to the world.

Overcoming negativity and fear

Are things really so bad?

The next time you are tempted to feel sorry for yourself, remember a few things.

You're alive and well. Many people are no longer around, and many others are in such poor health they can barely function. Yet every day, people with severe handicaps accomplish great things. If you are healthy and able-bodied, then you really have no excuse not to be the very best you can be.

Opportunities come disguised as problems. Problems are a blessing, because when you solve them you grow as a person and you gain valuable experience. You learn things that can allow you to help other people solve the same problem. If the problem you solve is big enough and widespread enough, the opportunity which it creates could be enormous.

Put your problems in perspective. Ask yourself what's the worst thing that can happen. Then accept that and move on past your problem.

Challenge is one of the best things you can face. Challenges and problems give you a chance to develop your resourcefulness. Problems are your opportunity to give it all you've got — to truly shine as a person.

Wouldn't it be great?

Wouldn't it be great if everything always went according to plan? If you always got your way? If everyone agreed with you? If you could easily have all the things you wanted? Wouldn't that be an ideal life?

As great as that might seem, the reality is that things do not always go according to plan, we don't always get our way, other people often think differently, and most things worth having are difficult to come by.

Is that so bad, though? I think not. If things always went according to plan, there would be no pleasant surprises. In fact, we'd likely get stuck in a rut. Some of the most delightful experiences come when we get sidetracked.

What can we learn from someone who always agrees with us? Not much. The varied opinions of others help us to grow in our own knowledge.

And the true value of anything is in the effort that goes into getting it. The things that come easy are usually of little value, regardless of what the price tag says. It's what you put into it that matters.

The happiest people are not those who always get their way, but rather those who make the most of what they've been handed.

The power of negative thinking

Let's be honest about it. Life is scary. I know, you're supposed to be a grown up and you're not supposed to be afraid of anything. But at three in the morning, when you're laying awake, unable to sleep because you're worrying about where you're going to get the money for the house payment, life can be frightening.

And sometimes, it can be very useful to admit that. Most of the time, we keep a "stiff upper lip." We try to maintain a positive attitude, to think that things will always get better. And there is much value in that. But there come times when you just need to deal with all the nagging little negative thoughts that build up as a result of your attempt to be positive all the time.

You know you have doubts all the time. You're often afraid to admit them even to yourself, but they're there. They eat away at you because you never let them out. Actually, negative feelings are healthy. They temper your enthusiasm with a dose of reality, and remind you that there are risks in everything you do. They help you remember to be careful. But if they build up inside of you, and are never dealt with, then they can immobilize you.

So every now and then, when you're feeling particularly blue, it's time to have an out-an-out bitching and moaning session. And if you raise such an event to the status of a ritual, that is, if you intentionally decide to do it, it can be very productive and beneficial to you.

Give it a try. Sit down and think about one of the problems in your life. Really dwell on it. Think of all the reasons why it makes your hopes and dreams and goals impossible to accomplish. In your mind, let your problem put a negative slant on every aspect of your life. Then, start having some fun with it. Start with a little exaggeration. Add some melodrama, and maybe a little obscenity. Say to yourself something like, "The truth is, I can't stand your little business venture. I hate you for even thinking of it. I thought things were fine just the way they were. I'm really too lazy to bother with all of it. I think I'll just eat a lot of chocolate and get fat."

You get the idea. Really revel in your misery to the point where it becomes funny. And you'll notice that your energy level starts to go up. Because negativity is energy, and it can get you moving when you let it come out. Have you ever seen a healthy two year old who lacks energy? Of course not. Because two year olds know something that we have forgotten — the value of a good tantrum.

If you keep your doubts and negative feelings bottled up inside, they eventually gain control of you. But letting them out in a good tantrum puts you back in the driver's seat. Acknowledging your problems and your doubts gives you control over them. Getting furious about them will give you the energy you need to overcome them.

So every now and then, think negative. It could have a very positive influence on your life.

Are you your own worst enemy?

Who talks you out of more things than anyone else? Your spouse? Your parents? Your boss? Your lawyer? If you're like most people, the answer probably is: yourself.

You have an "inner voice" that has opinions on everything you do. That inner voice has its own perspective on you as a person, and is acutely aware of your limitations and short-comings. Every time you attempt to step out of your box, to try something new and challenging, that inner voice starts in on you. "You can never do that," it says.

Well, that inner voice is wrong. You can do it if you set your mind to it, no matter what has happened in the past. In fact, your biggest obstacle is convincing yourself that you can. The first step in doing that is to acknowledge that the "inner voice" exists, and then take steps to counteract it.

The inner voice will always be there. You can't get rid of it. But you can keep it from dominating your thoughts and actions by supplying yourself with plenty of positive input.

Get yourself around positive, future-oriented people. Read books, listen to tapes, talk back to the voice and say, "Yes I can!" Dwell on the possibilities, not the risks. Model the behavior of successful people. Take action toward your goals. Remind yourself of your accomplishments and of the challenges you've overcome in the past. Write down your goals and review them at least once a day. Find your purpose in life keep yourself focused on it.

You can accomplish great things if you'll just let yourself do it.

Overwhelmed ?

Do you ever feel overwhelmed? There's so much that needs to be done, so many things pulling you down.

It can be discouraging and frustrating when you're being slowed down by things that are beyond your control. How do you cope?

The secret is — do what you can. You're not responsible for the things over which you have no control. Don't let them get you down. Instead, work to make improvements in your own life. Take control of the things that are your responsibility. Wisely use the resources you have, and don't waste your energy worrying about what you cannot change.

Everyone has challenges. Life itself is one big challenge. There are some things that we just can't change, that we must simply accept. Your acceptance will free up tremendous energy to tackle those things that you can change.

Make a difference where you can, and don't sweat the rest.

Fear of failure

Successful people know they cannot fail, because they know that there is no such thing as failure — there are only results. The achievers in this world are able to take action because they simply don't believe in failure.

Are you afraid of failure? Then you need to understand that there is no such thing as failure. You never fail — you always succeed in producing results. If you don't like the results you are producing, then you just have to find someone who is producing the results that you desire, and do the same things that that person is doing.

Belief in failure drags you down. If you believe that you have failed, then it affects your self-image and your ability to the things you want to do.

Remind yourself that failure is not an option. Everything you do has a result. If the things you are doing are not producing the results you desire, then change what you are doing. It is as simple as that. Don't dwell on your "failure." Think instead about what you could do differently to get the results you want.

Realize that you cannot fail, and you'll be able to do, to be, to have whatever you want.

Overcoming the fear of rejection

Does the fear of rejection keep you from taking the actions necessary to achieve your dreams? Imagine for a moment the kind of success you could have if you could transcend that fear.

Ask yourself, what's the worst that could happen if you are "rejected". Usually, the worst that can happen is that you'll hear someone say "no". Is that so bad?

Let your fear of rejection be a positive influence. Fear gives you energy, and the ability to sharply focus on your situation. So feel the fear, take energy and clarity from it, and do the feared thing anyway. Don't let your fear stop you, but let it motivate you to be more prepared.

Learn to transcend your fear by practice. Seek out "rejection" and experience it. Start small, with things that are inconsequential. Call a busy friend and invite her to lunch on short notice. Chances are, she'll say "no, thank you" and you'll have a "rejection experience" under your belt. Make a game out of it, trying to see how many "rejections" you can get before you get a "yes." With each experience, you'll gain a personal understanding that rejection is not "the end of the world" and that it is nothing to be feared.

Realize that you, and you alone, are responsible for your own worth. Nothing anyone can do, say or think will change your value as a human being. Only you have the power to do that. It is impossible for anyone to reject you unless you let them, because rejection occurs in your own mind.

Believe in what you're doing. That will make rejections the other person's problem, not yours.

Colonel Harlan Sanders was a retiree receiving Social Security. He had a pretty good recipe for fried chicken, and decided to try to sell the recipe to restaurants in return for a percentage of the revenue that it generated. Colonel Sanders drove around the country, sleeping in his car, looking for restaurants that might be interested in his recipe. He was rejected 1,009 times before someone finally said "yes". One thousand and nine rejections! Yet because he was able to keep going after each one, he made a fortune as the founder of Kentucky Fried Chicken.

Don't let the fear of rejection stop you. Learn to draw strength from it.

Risk and Fear

There are risks and costs to a program
of action, but they are far less than
the long-range risks and costs of
comfortable inaction.
— John F. Kennedy

It's interesting that many people who would never think of taking any risk in the pursuit of their dreams, risk their lives on a daily basis by driving too fast, not wearing seat belts, drinking too much, eating fattening food, or smoking cigarettes. If you're going to take risks, you might as well make them count. And if you're alive, you're taking some kind of risk.

Risks are absolutely necessary. Unless you're willing to take risks, and to fail miserably, and pick yourself back up to try again, success won't come to you. We must learn to take the necessary, calculated risks and avoid the foolish risks.

Driving drunk, without a seat belt on, and speeding — that's a foolish risk. Occasionally speeding to the airport to make a plane, or to an appointment because you've been delayed by other urgent business — those are calculated risks. There are times when you must take calculated risks.

If you have not yet reached your dream, then it's because there is some risky activity in the way. Something that you fear sits between you and your dream. The best way around your fear of anything is to confront it head on. It's simple, but very difficult. And absolutely necessary. When you do the thing you fear, your fear begins to fade, and soon it has no place in your life.

Going forward

Have you ever been so far down that you don't see how you can ever get out of it? Do you have problems that seem to overwhelm you? How do you come back from something like that? How do you move forward with your life?

Just remember this. No matter what has happened in the past, you always have something to contribute to life. As long as you are breathing, you can make a difference. It doesn't matter who you are or what you have been, or even what you have done. That is all in the past, and you cannot change it, but you can change the present and the future.

You can resolve to make a positive contribution to life — to your own life, to the lives of others, to your community, to the world, to the future. Nothing can pull you down far enough when you are resolved to make a difference, when you are committed to making a contribution.

Go forward. Find what you can contribute to life, and you will find fulfillment, joy and peace.

It is darkest just before dawn

I wonder how many people give up just when success is almost within reach. They persevere day after day, and just when they're about to make it, decide they can't take any more.

The difference between enormously successful people and miserable failures is not that much. Successful people have simply learned the value of staying in the game until it is won. Those who never make it are the ones who quit too soon.

Commitment means doing whatever it takes. Whatever it takes — not whatever is most comfortable. When things are darkest, and the storm clouds are gathering around, successful people stick with it because they know they're almost there.

The mountain is steepest at the summit, but that's no reason to turn back. You've made it this far. Keep going a little longer and you'll see the sun rise on a beautiful new day.

The Daily Motivator To Go

Feeling down?

Everyone has disappointments, setbacks, bad breaks and frustrations. Sometimes it seems that they all come at once, and we find ourselves in a funk. Suddenly we start to see the negative side of everything, and that is certainly no way to live. Let's look at some ways to quickly bounce back.

Take action. Do something positive. Even if it's just mowing the yard, or cleaning the old files from your hard disk. Taking action puts you in control of your life, and helps you to get positively focused. Small accomplishments can do wonders for your attitude.

Help someone else. Cheerfully do something for another person. Read a book to a child. Make a donation of time or money. Help your neighbor with a project. Give of yourself and you'll feel great.

Count your blessings. There are so many good things about life, and too often we take them for granted. Appreciate and be thankful for your home, your health, your family, your life's experiences, your friends, your skills, your knowledge, and the beautiful world around you. Think of all the people who love you and care about you.

Find a challenge. Re-direct your negative energy and frustrations toward something that will challenge you to be your best.

Things are as negative or as positive as you make them. Adjust your attitude and keep your life on the upward trail.

Mistakes

Everyone makes mistakes. They're nothing to be ashamed of. The only people who don't make mistakes are those who don't try to do anything. Being wrong is perfectly normal and routine.

The best thing to do when you make a mistake is to admit it — to yourself and to everyone else involved. Deal with it quickly and move on. Mistakes are excellent teachers, and to learn from mistakes you must first admit them. Clinging to a mistaken position will never make you right, and will just waste your time and energy. Mistakes are not good or bad, they're simply steps on the path to success.

Discovering that something DOESN'T work is just as valuable as discovering something that does work. So mistakes are actually very positive. The key is to learn from them, so you don't repeat them.

Thomas Edison tried thousands of ways to construct the electric light bulb before he finally got it right. Successful people in any field are not necessarily the best and the brightest. They're the ones with the most commitment — the ones who pick themselves up after every mistake and try again.

Use your mistakes for all they're worth. Keep trying, keep going, and do whatever it takes to get where you want to be.

You can do it

When the going gets rough, and it seems like you just cannot take any more, remember — you can take it, you can make it, you can do it.

All it ever takes is one step. One step in the direction of your goal. One step away from your troubles. Just one step. And then after that step, another. Anyone can take one step. You can take one step, right now.

You won't do it all in one day. It will take time. But you can do it. You can get anywhere you want to go, by just moving toward it every chance you get. Little steps, one after another, will get you there. Don't waste your time figuring out how to make big leaps. Just keep taking the small steps — they'll get you there more reliably and probably quicker.

Once you take that first step, and commit to taking the rest, things change. Momentum is suddenly on your side. What one step can you take right now, that will lead you toward the life you want? What one small thing can you do?

Do it now. And then, immediately look for the next step. Keep going until you're there.

Frustration

Are you frustrated? Great! Frustration will give you energy to change your life for the better. Achievement comes from people who are frustrated, not from those who are content.

Many people must first "hit bottom" before they have enough desire and motivation to change their lives. The more dissatisfied you are, the more energy you have to make things better.

Frustration is your way of telling yourself that you want things to change. Use the energy of your frustration to get excited. Take action. Don't let it get you down. Change it into a positive influence. Do something about it.

You're frustrated because you know things can be better, and you're ready to make them better. That's a signal that its time to take action. Feel your frustration, and get busy doing something about it.

What's the worst that could happen?

There's something that you really want to do. There is a person that you really want to be, deep inside. There is a life that you really want to live.

Go for it! Start today, taking action that will bring you to where you want to be. Are there any good reasons not to? Of course there are, but does that really matter?

If you're hesitant to take action, ask yourself this: What's the worst thing that can happen? Is failure the worst thing that can happen? No. Absolutely not. Each undesired result is just one more step toward your goal. Is success the worst that can happen? No. Of course not. Success is what you're after. So what is the worst thing that can happen?

Nothing. Doing nothing is the worst thing that can happen. When you take action, you are sure to get results, and eventually you will get the results you desire. When you take no action, you are assured of getting nowhere — a wasted life.

The only way to avoid the worst thing that can happen, is to take action. Do it now. Live the life you want to live by doing what needs to be done.

Acceptance

Do you ever have one of those days when nothing seems to go right? Disappointment piles on top of frustration. One little thing goes wrong, and you mentally start to fight it. Once you've got that attitude, frustration keeps cropping up everywhere.

Your frustration is not the result of external events. It is your feelings about those events, that cause you to be frustrated. Because you are the source of your own frustration and anxiety, you can make it vanish, too.

The key is acceptance. It breaks the downward spiral of frustration. Accept the moment for what it is. No person or thing is attempting to frustrate you — that's just the reaction you're having. Accept what is, without a fight, and you'll have the energy to make a positive change in the situation.

Don't Fight It

When you fight against something negative, you use most of your energy just to stay even. Little, if any, energy is remaining to help you get ahead. Even if you win, you lose.

Instead, work to re-direct negative energy and influences into a positive direction. It is not as difficult as it sounds. Love and hate are just across the border from each other. Anger and inspiration are separated by a thin line.

The same raw energy creates sadness as well as joyful bliss. Just as electricity can be used to make a room very warm or very cold, so too can the energy of life be used to manifest seemingly "opposite" results.

The energy is there. And it is up to you to decide what it will become. Don't fight it. Accept it, and find a way to use it.

Courage

It is natural to fear the unknown. For thousands of years, a healthy fear of the unknown has kept people alert enough to survive. Yet the fear must not keep us from marching ahead. We must have the courage to live and grow.

Courage is not the absence of fear. Rather, courage is the ability to act in the face of fear. Fear helps us by making us alert to danger. And with courage we use that heightened state of energy to meet our greatest challenges.

There is risk in everything we do. And often, there is even greater risk in doing nothing. Fear rightly keeps us from acting foolishly on some occasions. Other times, we must feel the fear, and do it anyway. We must have the courage and the confidence to turn a risk into an opportunity.

Your greatest achievements are waiting, just on the other side of your greatest fears.

When bad things happen

Just when things are the worst, is when you can make the most difference. When everything is going against you, is the best time to take positive action that will get things going for you.

The best cure for discouragement is action. Don't just sit there feeling sorry for yourself, do something! You got into this situation. You can get yourself out, and move forward to a life of success and achievement. It all starts when you begin to take control of your own destiny. Realize that your actions determine your future.

Haven't you had enough already? Start working your way out, right now. Some of life's greatest accomplishments come when positive action is taken in the midst of a discouraging situation.

What can you do today, right now, that will move you forward? Set your sights on the future and do it now.

There is always something

There is always something you can do. Whatever sadness, or obstacle or challenge or desperate situation you face, the best course is to do something about it. Whatever you can. No matter how small. Do something.

It may not seem like much, but it is critically important. It may not improve the situation, but it will improve you. As long as you are doing something, you have control over your life. Wishing for what might have been, or dwelling on how unfair it all is, will not get you anywhere.

Taking action puts you in control. By taking action, you refuse to let it get you down. It will still be painful and difficult, but you can handle it, you can get through it, when you decide to do something.

Maximum performance

Getting it done

The accepted wisdom is that we must work hard to get ahead. But that's not really true. It doesn't really matter how hard you work. What matters is how much you get done. Many people fall into the trap of doing a lot of work without ever getting anything done.

How does one get out of that trap? You start by learning to value yourself and your time. You must believe that your are a worthwhile, valuable individual with something unique to contribute to the world. When you adopt that mind-set, you'll realize what a shame it is to waste your time. You'll want to find ways to be more productive because you'll value your own time so highly. Among those ways to be more productive:

Learn to say no. Unfortunately, people will take advantage of you if you let them. If they know that you'll do their work for them, then they'll let you. If they're doing something equally valuable in return, that's no problem. The problem comes when they start to take advantage of you. In the long run, no one benefits. You get bogged down in unproductive activity, and they develop a dependency mind-set. For your sake and theirs, learn to say no — firmly and politely.

Deal with things as they come up. Problems don't go away by themselves — they just get worse. If you don't deal with things immediately, you waste time worrying about them. And by the time you get around to dealing with them, it usually takes more time and effort than if you had handled it earlier.

Keep focused. There are hundreds of distractions that can knock you off task. Find a way to focus on your goals. Write them down and review them several times a day. More importantly, find a reason behind what you're doing. When you're confident of what you're doing, and of why you're doing it, you will stay focused.

Never stop learning. Always be on the lookout for new ways to do something. Just because you've done something the same way for 3 years doesn't mean that's the best way to do it. Step outside your box and look for new and different ways to work.

Remember — it's not how hard you work, it's how much you get done that counts. Keep yourself focused on what needs to be done, and you'll get to where you want to be.

Are you too busy to do anything?

How many times do you hear yourself say it. "I'm too busy to do anything." Have you ever thought about what that means — literally? If you're too busy to do anything, then what are you busy doing?

Think back on all the things you've accomplished, and on all the things you hoped to accomplish but didn't. Where did all the time go? Every day you wake up with a full day ahead of you, with plenty of time to work toward your goals. Then at the end of the day you often feel that you haven't gotten any closer. What happened?

Chances are, you were too busy. Being busy does not get anything done. Being busy just uses time. Take a look at how you spend your time. Ask yourself why you're doing the things you do. Ask yourself if what you're doing is moving you in the direction of your goals. Look at your activities with the goal of making the best use of your time. Learn to say no to activities that just keep you busy but don't help you to accomplish anything.

Attitude can play a big part. If you take the attitude that you're trying to "just get through the day" that's exactly what you'll do — just get through the day. When you adopt the mind-set of "let's see how much I can accomplish today" then you'll get a lot more done.

Turn negative energy into personal power

Imagine for a moment that you are very powerful and highly effective. You have considerable resources at your disposal, and you know how to use them to solve problems and accomplish your objectives.

How would you act today if that were the case? Would you let every little setback get you down? Or would you use your enormous power and influence to quickly and effectively deal with every situation? Would your attitude be one of frustration and resignation, or would you be charged with excitement, energy and enthusiasm?

You're on your way back from lunch and there's a signal light malfunction that has traffic backed up for several blocks. No one is moving anywhere.

If you see yourself as a frustrated, tired, overworked victim, this incident will be additional confirmation to you that the world is unfair. You'll probably blow your horn to let off steam, and curse at the other drivers, all the time raising your blood pressure and giving yourself a lot of heavy negative energy.

If, however, you see yourself as powerful and effective, you'll use the opportunity to listen to an educational audiotape — one you've been saving for just such an occasion. Our you'll use your cell phone to return calls, and possibly even do some prospecting.

The same "reality" happens to everyone. It is how we chose to react that makes the difference between a miserable failure and a smashing success. You have the power to direct all your energy toward achievement and fulfillment of your dreams. That power comes from the way you choose to look at life.

When you see every situation as an opportunity, when you quit complaining and use your time to get things done, then you will be powerful and effective. Anger and frustration create a great amount of energy, but so does an atomic bomb. The key to success is to harness that energy. Re-direct it toward positive action and accomplishment.

A little bit more

When things get difficult, that's the time to give it your all. That's when you can make the biggest difference.

It is when you reach the edge of your abilities, and you come face to face with your limitations, that you begin to grow. When you are forced to push yourself beyond the limit, you will raise yourself above the crowd.

Give it all you've got, and then give it a little bit more. That little bit will make all the difference. That little bit will turn struggle into achievement. It only takes one point more than the other team, to win the Super Bowl. It only takes a few hundredths of a second less than the nearest runner, to win the race.

Making the effort will keep you in the race. Giving a little bit extra on top of that, will make you a winner.

Creativity is a balancing act

As the pace of life becomes faster, as markets become more segmented, as tools become more sophisticated, and as individuals become more interconnected, the need for creativity is greater than ever before.

Creativity has two distinct processes, and each one is vital.

First is the process of integration and synthesis of a new idea. Everything new that is created — great buildings, works of art, businesses, complex machines, books, films — must first exist in the mind. New ideas come largely from the integration of existing concepts — combining and intermingling them in ways that have never before been expressed. This part of the creative process requires exposure to a diverse set of experiences and a broad spectrum of thinking.

Just as vital to creativity is the action necessary to bring ideas to reality. The creation of great architecture demands engineering and construction skills. The creation of great literature demands grammatical skills, and the ability to operate a printing press. Discipline and focus are necessary to manifest any creation.

It's a bit of a paradox. In order to be fully creative, we must be very open-minded, while at the same time remaining disciplined and focused. A delicate balance, indeed. And balance is the key. In all great creations the idealistic coexists with the pragmatic in an elegant proportion. A great idea is worthless unless it is manifest. And a great skill is useless unless it has direction.

Think balance. Learn to be a dreamer while also being a doer. Harness the power of your thoughts and the power of your actions together in the same direction, and your life will be a truly creative force.

How do you spend your time?

Time is the most precious and limited thing you have. It is something that everyone has in an equal amount each day. The difference between a life of fulfillment and abundance, and a life of mediocrity, is determined by how you spend your time. It is as simple as that.

Treat every moment as the precious gift that it is. Use your time to build and create and accomplish. Don't waste your time with envy, sloth, anger and regret. In everything you do, ask yourself: is it worth spending an irreplaceable part of my life on this?

Time can work for you if you learn to use it wisely. Consistent and focused effort, over time, will bring desired results. Remember that each moment is an opportunity that must be taken now.

A little something extra

You never know when that little something extra might make a big difference in the end. Races are won by hundredths of a second, and there are countless opportunities along the way to gain the slight edge that will make all the difference.

Everyone puts out maximum effort when the finish line is

in sight. Only the true winner knows that the race is not won at the end, but rather along the way. In fact, the true winner starts to win long before the race is even begun, by putting a little something extra into each training session.

A slight edge, every step of the way, will add up to a big advantage in the end. What can you do today, to improve your performance just a little bit over what you did yesterday? What little bit extra can you do for your boss, your spouse, your children, your customers, your friends, yourself? It adds up, until it is unstoppable. Just a little something extra, every day. Think about the power of that.

Raise your standards

The best way to keep from falling back, is to constantly move ahead. If you truly want a better life, then live it! Look for ways to grow, in every area of your life. Continue to raise your expectations, and your standards.

Raise your standards in the work you do. Look for ways to provide additional value. Explore new techniques for working more efficiently and effectively. Question everything you do, and consider ways to do it better.

Raise the standards of the people you're with. If you're hanging out with whiners and complainers, they'll drag you down. Get around people who can inspire and challenge you.

Raise your health standards. No one should be sick and tired all the time. No matter what your age, you can feel great and have abundant energy if you'll commit to taking care of your body. Feed yourself real, nutritious food, drink lots of water, exercise every day and get plenty of rest.

Raise the standards in the way you spend your time. Live life on purpose. Things like envy, regret, and revenge waste your precious time and accomplish nothing. Use your time to make positive contributions to your own life and the lives of others.

Raise your standards. You want a better life? Great! Make it better in all you do.

Recovery time

Everyone has setbacks. The key to successfully dealing with them is to recover quickly and get back on track.

Sure, there's a tendency to feel sorry for yourself, to complain, and to imagine all the terrible things that can happen. These things may feel good in some strange way, and they're useful in moderation. But they won't get you where you're going.

The longer you take to mentally recover from your setbacks, the worse you make them. You can't prevent negative things from happening, but you can decide how much power they will have over your life.

When you experience a setback, put it in perspective. It won't look so bad when viewed in the overall context of your life. Look for ways to turn the problem into an opportunity. Maybe other people experience the same problem. Look for what you can learn from it. There's almost always some positive aspect to everything. And make adjustments so that it won't happen again. Take positive action instead of continuing to feel sorry for yourself.

It helps if you have a clear direction and focus, and a plan of action for your life. Then, instead of wallowing in self pity when setbacks come, you can get right back to work and leave them far behind.

Yes, but...

The word "but" is a killer. It kills your dreams. It gives you an endless supply of reasons to live a life of desperation and mediocrity.

"Yes, I'd like to go back to school, but I just can't find the time."

In life, there are either results or there are excuses. Unfortunately, most of us have too many excuses and not enough results. Excuses are worthless. Why do we even bother with them? They make us "feel" better, they allow us to deceive ourselves, they help us to forsake responsibility for our own lives.

"I want to, but... I need to, but... I could be, but..." But what?

To make something of your life, you need to bust some "buts". Get rid of them. For starters, replace "but" with "and". That just naturally makes things more open ended.

"Yes, I'd like to go back to school, and...

...and here's how I'm going to do it."

"But" may make you feel better in the short run by providing justification for your lack of action. Eventually, though, your "buts" become a crutch. "But" is an escape, that too soon becomes a trap.

Go for the results. Forget the excuses.

Less is More

Do you find that you never have enough time to do everything that needs to be done? Did you ever consider that you could get more done with less effort? There's no such thing as something for nothing. However, there is no need to ever use more than the minimum effort necessary.

The less effort you put into getting each thing accomplished, the more you'll be able to do. Reducing your effort is not being lazy — far from it. In fact, it could be argued that NOT working to become more efficient is the lazy way to live. When you look for ways to reduce your efforts, you'll open your eyes to a whole new way of doing things.

For example, it takes less effort to regularly change your car's oil, than to replace the engine. It takes less effort to put things away when you're finished with them, than to trip over them every time you walk through the room. It takes less effort to deal with a problem early, than to avoid it and have it grow bigger. It takes less effort to save in advance for a purchase, than to buy it on credit and pay the interest. It takes less effort to do it NOW, than to ponder it, and worry about it, and wonder if you should, and then play catch up because it took you so long to get started. It takes less effort to do the difficult tasks early in the day, when your mind is fresh and clear, than to stay up late and do them while fighting fatigue.

With each thing you undertake, ask "How can I do this with less effort?" There is usually a way, and by finding it you will grow vastly more effective.

Bring out the best

How do you bring out the best in others? By doing your best.

A teacher brings out the best in his students by giving his best in the classroom. A salesperson brings out the best in his clients by giving the best possible service and attention. A manager brings out the best in her employees by setting and example of diligent, consistent work.

And it works in every direction. Employees bring out the best in their employers by doing their best possible work. Students bring out the best in their teachers when they are fully committed to learning.

The people around you are a reflection of you. If you're focused, responsible and full of energy you'll find that the people around you will be the same way. People naturally tend to relate with you on your own wavelength. Your attitude is contagious.

Think of how you'd like people to be, and then be that way yourself. It all starts with you.

Never Stop Learning

The one thing in life that can never be taken away from you is your education. You can lose your money, your home, your job, and even your family. You can never lose the things you learn.

Education is not just what you learn in school, not by a long shot. Unfortunately, many people make the mistake of "finishing" their education when they graduate. And education is not just learning facts. Education is learning how to learn on a continuing basis.

It is more important than ever that you never stop learning. With the rapid advances in knowledge and technology, information quickly becomes obsolete. So you must learn not only the facts, but more importantly, how to find the information you need.

If you are not continually updating your knowledge you will be left behind. You must always be looking for a better way to do something, for the knowledge that will make you more effective. Because you can be sure that your competition is doing just that.

Learn to learn... to be innovative

The median length of a career in the United States is only six years. That means that 50% of the people in the U.S. change careers every six years. That's careers, not just jobs.

It used to be that people could go to school, learn a trade, and work hard in that field until retirement. The world just doesn't work that way any more. And isn't that an incredible opportunity — for individuals, for businesses, for innovation and for society.

The opportunity comes at a price, though — the suffering of those who are displaced from work by rapidly changing technology and innovation. Whole industries are sometimes lost virtually overnight. Look at what happened to the vinyl record industry when music CDs came along.

You owe it to yourself, to your family, to your community to be a lifelong learner. For it is the willingness to learn and adopt new things that will enable you to take advantage of the incredible opportunities of the future. This is an attitude you'll want to adopt in every area of your life. Innovation can add value to everything you do — look for new ways to be entertained, to eat, to communicate, to handle financial transactions, to travel, to exercise, to serve others, and of course, to learn. Seek out innovation and you'll find something useful almost every day.

Watch and imitate

Do you want to be successful in any particular undertaking? Then find someone else who has done it, and do exactly what they did. Model your actions on successful experience.

Successful people are not simply lucky. Luck has nothing to do with it. Success comes from specific actions, taken in a specific way. Winners make it look easy, and effortless, but it is not. Behind every successful person is a long line of effort, a specific sequence of actions.

Discover what those actions are, repeat them, and you too can have the same result. Don't waste your time directing envy or resentment toward successful people. Instead, be curious. Find out all you can. Ask questions. Read books and articles. Listen. Observe. Learn from the experience of those who have reached the top, and you'll be on your way there.

Balance

A good, productive day of work enables you to have a great rest at night. A great rest at night enables you to have a good, productive day of work.

Life is a cycle of effort and rest. The effectiveness of each depends on the other. You cannot cheat this cycle. Sleep all night and day and you'll feel awful. Work (or play) all day and night and you'll be worthless the next day.

Maximum effectiveness requires balance. You've got to work hard, and you've got to stop along the way to rest and relax. Sometimes you can be more effective in your work, by doing less of it. Sometimes you can get a better rest, when you work a little harder.

Try to drive your car with only three tires, and you'll appreciate the need for balance. Get out of balance, and nothing works right. To live effectively, you must have balance — in your diet, in your schedule, in your relationships, in your ideas, in your viewpoints. If you go too far out in one direction, you could topple over.

Think balance, and get the most from life.

Joyful downtime

It is important to have joy in your life on a regular basis. Working hard and being responsible is great. And you need to have fun, too.

What do you have to look forward to? To get excited about doing?

Think about how productive and motivated you are on the day before you leave to go on vacation. In such a situation you know two things: (1) You MUST get your work done now, because after today you'll be gone for two weeks, and (2) Nothing can get you down, because tomorrow you'll be on vacation.

What if you could work like that every day? You can, if you regularly take time to just enjoy life. Give yourself some time to look forward to.

Find something you enjoy for its own sake — not because it will give you a networking opportunity, not because you will learn something, not because it will set a good example for your kids, not because it will look good on your resume, not because it will improve your social standing. Find something joyful that you can do without any reason or expectation other than just pure enjoyment. Something that will get you excited and motivated. Then set aside time and do it, without guilt. You deserve it. It will balance your life, and make you more effective in everything you do.

What's holding you back?

What things are holding you back, preventing you from reaching your full potential? We tend to avoid thinking about

The Daily Motivator To Go

such things, because they can be painful. Or we blame our troubles and lack of progress on someone else. Avoiding the real issue may "feel" better at the moment. Yet it does nothing to move us forward.

The moment you honestly and clearly face your limitations, you begin to transcend them. Yes, it involves effort to work on your shortcomings. In the end, though, it will be less effort than you would spend continually working against them.

Discovering your limitations gives you a powerful opportunity to be more effective. Once you remove something that's holding you back, you're finished fighting it. That gives you more energy to put into achieving your goals.

Take a good, hard look at your fears, your assumptions, your weaknesses. Admit them, and put your effort into overcoming them. It will pay a lifetime of dividends.

Endurance

Many things we can change, and some things we must endure. We grow by our endurance. Strength comes from adversity.

Often, the things we want to have in life, lie on the other side of hardship. We must pass through times of difficulty and extreme effort in order to reach our goals. Almost anything worth having is not easily obtained, and the effort involved is what gives it value.

Endurance allows us to get where we're going. The higher the goal, the longer and more arduous the path. The more endurance we can muster, the more we can achieve.

Clearly seeing the end of the path, and keeping the goal in sight, makes endurance possible. We can hold up under amazing difficulty, when we know there's a purpose.

Keep your chin up, look forward, and endure what you must. It will make you what you want to be.

Feedback

Always seek and consider honest feedback from others. When you see your strengths and weaknesses through the eyes of others, you get a clearly defined path for improvement. And continued improvement will lead you to success.

Everyone who is now at the top, started out at the bottom. Every large, successful company was once a start-up operation. They all moved from the bottom to the top, through continual improvement.

Success depends on providing value to others. So it is crucial to know exactly how other people perceive the value you offer. Every day you have the opportunity to make incremental improvements in your work. Good, honest feedback from those who are affected by that work, will show you how to do that. It's a valuable resource that can move you ahead.

Try something different

Never has it been more important, or more interesting, or more fulfilling, to be open minded and curious. The world is changing at an explosive pace. The winners in today's world are those who can recognize and embrace new ideas and concepts, while maintaining a strong, continuing foundation of life values.

The older and more experienced you get (and we're all headed in that same direction), the more you're in danger of becoming closed minded. When you've seen it all, you begin to think like you've seen it all, acting out of habit and preconceived notions.

Experience is a wonderful teacher. Don't let your past experience limit you, though. Experience is best used, when it is continually renewed and updated.

Make an effort to keep your mind open. Try something new today. Do something in a different way. Meet a new person. Turn down an unexplored road. Consider an opposing opinion. Read a magazine that's completely out of your field.

There's a whole world out there, that wasn't even in existence yesterday. Don't miss it!

What results are you getting?

In the end, it really doesn't matter what you're doing, or how you feel, or what you think. Eventually, it comes down to this. What results are you getting?

What are the numbers? How much money are you putting in the bank? How fast can you run 10 kilometers? What's your cholesterol? What grades are you getting? How many sales are you making? How many chapters have you written? How many people in your downline? How many games has your team won? How many members does your church have? Did you get enough votes to win?

On a regular basis, you need to review your results and compare them against your goals. The big thing you need to ask is this — are you heading in the right direction? Are you moving toward the results you want?

If so, that's great. You know you're doing the right things.

If not, then it's really good to find out that you need to change what you're doing. This isn't all that complicated, yet some folks just can't seem to figure it out. If you're not getting the results you want, then you need to change what you're doing.

Focus is necessary. Action is necessary. Motivation is necessary. Self esteem is necessary. Knowledge is necessary. Commitments is necessary. Discipline is necessary. However, these are not enough. Results are what count.

There is no question but that you are getting results. The question is, are they the results you want? And the answer to that question is not "well..." or "I think maybe..." or "if only I could..." The answer is either "yes" or "no". It doesn't get much simpler than that.

Accomplishment endures

What will you do today, that will matter tomorrow? Excitement and thrills fade, and become fond memories. Pleasure and comfort become monotonous. What endures? Accomplishment. Get something done today, something that makes a difference, and you'll reap the benefits for a long time to come.

Accomplishment brings many things: money, satisfaction, confidence, skills, respect, influence, knowledge, and more. These are things that last long after you're finished. And they'll help you to build one accomplishment on top of another, on top of another, and so on.

As you go about your day, there will be things you need to do, things you want to do, things you absolutely must do. Remember, in all your doing, the value of accomplishment. Shift your focus from what you're doing, to what you're getting done. What comes from all your activity? What are you accomplishing? What are you building, collecting, creating, selling, distributing, managing, or improving? What are you accomplishing?

What will you have at the end of today, that you didn't have this morning? What actions will make that happen? When you just "get through" the day, and spend it in idleness, it will soon be gone. When you invest the day in accomplishment, it will always be with you.

Possibilities

Circles and Boundaries

Around every circle, a larger circle may be drawn. Around every fence, there is an open field that is waiting to be cultivated and harvested. Around every set of limitations, there is a limitless expanse of possibilities. Around every experience, there are larger and more meaningful experiences.

Beyond every horizon, there is a world of discovery. It is yours if only you will make it yours. A universe filled with abundance awaits you if you will just accept it.

When you are standing on the ground, the horizon is only a few miles away. On a mountain top, the horizon expands to dozens of miles. In an airplane, the horizon can be hundreds of miles away. In a spacecraft orbiting the Earth, there are thousands of miles between the horizons. And when you leave Earth orbit, the horizon is infinite. Where is your mind's horizon?

You can choose to bounce back and forth off the walls of your limitations, or you can choose to transcend those limitations and expand your horizons. You are only limited by the boundaries you place on yourself. Rise above your limitations, expand your thinking, and consider the possibilities.

You are full of possibilities

You are full of possibilities. No matter what your age, your education, your physical condition, or your financial situation, your life is filled with possibilities.

The frustration you feel, comes when these possibilities are not being realized. You're here to make a difference in your own special way. No one else can bring your own unique perspective to the world.

You can make a difference. And it will bring fulfillment to your life.

All the great human creations and achievements have been accomplished by people who are just like you. By people who chose to fulfill their possibilities. Everyone is special. Everyone has within them the potential for greatness. Choose to live your possibilities. Choose to make a difference, and no obstacle can hold you back.

Possibilities

What if you could see into the future?

Learn to recognize the possibilities in your life, and you'll see into your own future, in time to do something about it. Life is full of possibilities — some good, some bad. The better we become at recognizing and anticipating them, the more effective and successful we will be.

There are countless opportunities that pass you by because you never even know about them. And there are all too many unpleasant "surprises" that could have been avoided, had you seen them coming. When you pay attention to the possibilities, you have more options, more control in your life.

To increase your possibility awareness, you must first accept your current situation. Resist the temptation to complain, or blame, or deny, or to engage in wishful thinking about what "could have been". What is, is. Look at the reality of your situation. Detach yourself from the emotions of the moment. Though emotions can be a very powerful source of motivation, they can also blind you to reality. In order to see all the possibilities, you must be totally aware of the situation.

Next, open your mind. Consider new ideas, get out of your routine, read a magazine that's completely unrelated to anything you're interested in — see what the rest of the world is doing. You'll recognize possibilities much more readily when you're constantly challenging your assumptions.

Finally, act on the possibilities. When you see opportunity, take steps to make the most of it. If you see a possible danger or threat, take steps to protect yourself. Being able to say "I did something about it" is far more satisfying than just saying "I knew it."

Be open to possibilities. They're everywhere, and they are your future.

Here You Are

Your whole life has led to this moment. Everything you've done, all that you've been, and seen, and dreamed has led to where you are right now. The triumphs, the mistakes, the efforts, the fun, the losses — it has all brought you right here, right now.

You are, right now, where you have wanted to be. If you had truly wanted to be somewhere else, you would be there now. Your life is in your hands. You hold the key to the future, and it will be formed from your desire, your commitment and your actions.

You are your life. Your life is the expression of you. Everything that has filled your life has served to make you special. No one else can be the person you were meant to be. You are one of a kind, and it is up to you to make the most of your unique, living expression.

Look at what you've done

One good way to get a perspective on your life is to look at all the things you've accomplished. And don't think you haven't accomplished anything, because you have.

If you're alive and breathing then you've accomplished one thing for sure — survival. Chances are, you've done a lot more that you don't even think about. Stop for a moment and think about it. What things have you acquired that you always wanted? Perhaps a certain car, or a stereo system, or a computer. What kinds of experiences have you had. Think of all the enjoyable dinners eaten out, a hiking adventure, sporting events you've attended, trips, parties. Think of all the people you've met and formed relationships with — not just "romantic" relationships, but friendships, business contacts, social, political and artistic contacts.

Think of the books you've read, the skills you've learned, the things you've repaired, the films you've enjoyed, the record albums you've collected. These are all things you've accomplished. And of course don't forget the big accomplishments: jobs, formal education, wealth, children and other major things you've done in life.

Then truth is, when you think about it, your life has been full of accomplishments. Every day you get what you want much of the time. You've learned how to survive and to enjoy life. On a daily basis, you use your energy and your resources to accomplish things, both major and minor.

Now, consider for a moment what your life could be like if all that energy were directed toward a single purpose. You could literally do anything you wanted. The energy is already there. You prove that on a daily basis by all the things that you are able to accomplish. In order to reach your dream, the only thing you need to do is to FOCUS that energy toward the fulfillment of that dream.

We're all more accomplished than we think. Look at your life and see how far you've come. You'll realize that you DO know how to get what you want. Make the commitment to focus all that energy in a single direction, and the results will be awesome.

How many trees are in the seed?

A tiny seed becomes a tree. That tree produces many more seeds, which become trees, which produce seeds, and so on. So how many trees are in the seed?

There are no trees in the seed. Crack it open, and you won't find even a single tree. The seed contains only the idea of a tree, the potential for a tree, and the plans for building that tree. The tree itself appears only when the seed is nourished with water and soil and sunlight.

The people you meet, the new things you learn, the experiences you live, the choices you make, the days and moments of your life — all are seeds with limitless potential to bear fruit. But only when placed in fertile ground and nourished.

That's where you come in. Though you can't always control the seeds that fall into your life, you can control the way they're planted and cared for. In every moment is a lifetime of possibilities. Think of that! You can change the course of the rest of your life right now, this very instant. By deciding which seeds to plant, which choices to make, which relationships to nurture. By giving the seeds of opportunity a fertile soil in which to grow.

Imagine yourself

Imagine your perfect day. You are surrounded by the people you most enjoy and admire. You are in your favorite place. You are doing what you love to to, and you're very good at it. You have all the things you need to enjoy life, to be effective and fulfilled.

There is no limit to what you can imagine. And whatever you can imagine, you can become. Yet imagination is only the first step. To get there, action is also needed. Imagination will guide that action. Most of us are taking some kind of action all the time. We have no shortage of action. Without imagination though, many of our actions are wasted. Imagination will guide your actions in the direction of your dreams.

Imagine yourself being, doing, having whatever you want. See it vividly in all its detail. Feel it. Enjoy it. See it so completely and so realistically that you literally begin taking the actions necessary to get there.

Imagine yourself following every step along the way. Pay particular attention to the first step, because that's the one you need to be taking now... There, did you take that first step? Your imagination is well on its way to becoming reality.

Now move on to the second step. Your imagination can lead you there, as long as you do the walking.

Explore the possibilities

Think of all the incredible things that have come to pass, just because someone wondered "why?" or "why not?", or "what if?" Science, technology, philosophy, and civilization itself all benefit enormously from the spirit of exploration that is in every one of us.

Almost every situation is an opportunity for exploring possibilities. For asking why. For considering the many what ifs. For looking at how, and how much better can we make it.

Take the time and effort to explore the possibilities, and you gain control over your world. Everything happens for a reason, everything has a cause. And when you understand the cause, you can control the result. This is true whether you're debugging software, or planting a garden, or training your dog.

If life has you frustrated, that's great! There's enormous energy in that frustration. Just ask why, and why not, and what if. Soon, you'll be wrapped up in limitless possibilities.

The Best of Times

We live in a time of unprecedented opportunity. Free markets, increased political freedom, information technology, efficient transportation and distribution, innovations in the areas of management and human potential, and many other exciting, positive factors are at work in the world today.

Yes there is turmoil, because things are changing so rapidly. And with that chaos, comes opportunity. When things are no longer the way they've always been, there's a chance to make them better.

Never has there been a better time to be the person you are. Never has there been a better time to express your own unique perspective. Never has there been a better time to take advantage of innovation, and to create innovation.

Make the most of it — today, tomorrow, this month, this year. See the unlimited possibilities around you, and make the effort to turn them into incredible accomplishments. Each day is a golden opportunity that is filled with countless seeds of greatness. Abundance is all around you — make yourself a part of it.

Pathways to success

The True Secret to Success

Are you ready to learn the true secret to success? Success in anything: business, health, relationships, education — anything you desire. Success can be yours. You can be a winner today if you will simply take the time to learn and appreciate this one critical secret. It is a secret shared by all the successful people in the world.

The secret of success is. . . . .

There is no secret!

There is no secret to success. The way to success is there for all to see. It is not hidden in some obscure formula, something you can buy in a "special report" for only $49.95. Many people would like to think that such a thing exists, and many people spend lots of time and money trying to find a shortcut to success. The sad thing is, in the time they've spent looking for a shortcut, they could probably have already achieved success if they had just made the commitment at the outset to pay their dues.

So many people try so hard to make it big. But making it big is very, very difficult. It doesn't happen very often. That's why, when it happens, you hear about it. It's big news. But you don't hear about the millions of times people try to make it big and don't.

What we should be spending our time and effort doing is making it little. It's easy to do. Anyone can make a little improvement in what they are doing. And if you put your efforts into consistent, little improvements, soon they will add up and you will indeed have made it big. Try to make it big and you will spin your wheels; try to make little improvements and you will soon make it big.

Let's say you make your goal to improve your performance by 1% each day. That's easy, isn't it. If you spent an hour and a half on the phone today, calling people about your opportunity, then spend an hour and 31 minutes tomorrow. If you sent out 250 mailings last week, send out 253 this week. If you made $100 today, aim for $101 tomorrow. That's just one dollar more — what could be so hard about that? Go yourself one better — one percent better, that is. The secret is being dedicated and consistent about it. Soon, your efforts will compound as you begin improving on the improvements. If you try to earn 1% more each day, in just a little more than two months you will have doubled your income. And it just gets better and better as time goes on.

In six months, you will have increased your income 600%. In a year, if you were originally making $100 a day, you will be making more than $1.3 million a year simply by improving yourself by 1% per day. Let's carry this to the extreme and say you were actually able to continue to improve your income, just 1% per day, for a second year. At the end of the second year your income would be more than $52 million a year!

Maybe that's realistic, maybe it's not. There are people who earn that kind of money. Did they just get lucky? I don't think so. They got there by constant improvement, by refusing to accept things as they are, by dedicated and consistent effort.

But the point isn't whether or not you can earn $52 million a year. (And by the way, if you truly believe you can, you can.) The point is this. If you commit to continuous growth and improvement, if you implement a long-term, focused strategy, you will succeed in doing whatever it is you set about to accomplish. So what if you don't improve your 1% every single day. If you have that as your goal, then chances are that at the very least, you will not slide backward. At the very least, you will continue to stay even every day, to put forth the effort to reach your goals.

The Habit of Success

Habits are useful in that they keep us from having to concentrate on certain tasks that we repeat over and over again. Think of when you first learned to drive a car. You would really have to concentrate on every aspect of your driving. Now, after years of experience, driving has become a habit (hopefully a good one!). You don't have to think about it nearly as much. That's what we call learning.

Habits have their dark side, too. They can stifle your creativity, prevent you from taking advantage of new opportunities, and waste a lot of time and money. Habits like cigarette smoking, eating too much fat, and drinking too much alcohol or caffeine can be very harmful to your health.

The trick is to learn to control your habits — to get rid of the harmful ones and encourage the good habits that will take you in the direction of your goals. Most great accomplishments require consistent efforts over a long period of time. Developing the right habits will take care of the "consistent efforts" part. Time will take care of itself — it will continue to march forward whether you are going forward with it or not.

Getting rid of an undesirable habit takes a conscious effort. It is not easy. It is certainly possible, though, and with enough energy and desire can be accomplished. It is foolish to say that your habits control you — that is admitting defeat. Developing a good habit is difficult work, as well. Any parent knows how much effort and patience it takes to teach their child to brush his teeth twice a day, look both ways before crossing the street, wash his hands before eating, other things like that. It is not easy. It requires determination. And it is vitally important.

Next time you find yourself driving your car, with your seat belt buckled, think about how you got there. Do you remember putting on your seat belt? Hopefully, it is just an automatic motion that you do without thinking. And someday, it could save your life. It is just a little thing that takes almost no time — its power comes in the fact that you do it every time you get in the car. Ask yourself, what other habits can I develop that will allow me to consistently, automatically, move toward my goals?

Occasionally, people are able to take a shortcut to success. They get lucky, win the lottery, get in on a once-in-a-lifetime business deal, just happen to be in the right place at the right time. It does happen, but it is not a reliable path to success. Many people spend their whole lives just waiting for that lucky break. Buying those lottery tickets week after week, and never, ever winning. You don't hear about those people very often. They live lives of quiet desperation. They never end up being in the right place at the right time. Yet our culture encourages the "get rich quick" mentality because we make such a big deal about it when it happens. That is unfortunate.

For the vast majority of successful people, accomplishment comes one day at a time, little by little, day after day, month after month, year after year. That is the guaranteed way to success. It is the result of making a decision to abandon the harmful habits and replace them with the habits of success and accomplishment.

Make people feel needed

Remember always that people want to feel needed. They want to help out and be a part of what you are doing. When you satisfy this desire in people, you receive their admiration, loyalty, respect and cooperation.

Other people can be a powerful source of ideas, of motivation, of business contacts — if you encourage their participation. Most people are only too willing to help. Most people are genuinely flattered when you ask for their opinion or their expertise.

On the other hand, you must not take advantage of people. Asking someone for their help out of laziness on your part will not win you any points. People are willing to help you only if they see you are putting forth your own best effort. No one will want to help you if you don't help yourself. However, if you're striving toward excellence every day, people will jump all over themselves to be a part of what you are doing.

And always show sincere appreciation. People will want to help you only if they feel you are truly grateful.

There's an old story in the sales business about a salesman who doubled his orders for cash registers by asking for advice rather than orders. He would call on each prospect, introduce himself, and say, "Mr. Jones, I didn't come here to sell you a machine. I came to get some advice. I'm new at this and I wonder if you would show me how to sell it." The prospect would almost always be quite complimented, and work up a great sales presentation. Then the salesman would say, "You make it sound like you need one." He made many sales just from letting the other person take part.

This concept only works if you're willing to "give" as much as you "take." If you're always willing to help and advise others, then there will be plenty of people whom you, in turn, can call on for advice and assistance.

It's very, very difficult to accomplish anything alone. And it is quite unnecessary as well. There are plenty of people willing to help you if you will only ask.

Adjust your thinking for success

Here are five attitude adjustments for successful living. Keep them in mind as you go through your day.

• Act, don't react. When you react to something, you are not really in control of your own destiny. Reactions can be time-wasting distractions that keep you from what you really want to do. Taking action, taking the initiative, will prevent you from having to react.

• Remember that "those who know HOW will always work for those who know WHY." Look for the why, and see the big picture. There are always those who know HOW. The world rewards visionaries who can see the WHY.

• Stay focused. Jumping from thing to thing dilutes your skills, your enthusiasm and your time. You can have anything you want, but not everything. Decide what you really want and go for it. Learn to let go of the rest.

• Look for opportunity in all situations — especially problems. Every problem is positively ripe with opportunity. Opportunity is everywhere. Learn to open your eyes to it. Ask "How can I do this better? Why did this happen? What would prevent this problem from occurring in the future?"

• Look for ways to create value. Those who can deliver the most value to the most people are the winners in life.

Creative play

Knowledge and technology are advancing at such a rapid pace that we must always be learning new things. That means every day. It's a challenge, and a necessity. If you're not using the latest tools and techniques, your competition is, and you're falling behind.

But how can you keep up in such a fast-changing world?

The answer is to just try things. And the best way to do that is, be curious and have fun. Spend time playing. Playing creatively.

Look at small children and how they learn so much so fast. Their prime motivation is to have fun and to satisfy their endless curiosity. And the result is an astonishing amount of learning in a short period of time.

Take a look at that new software upgrade you just installed — the one that's loaded with new features. Don't just continue to use it the same way you used the old version. Try some of those new features, even if you don't have a practical use for them. Once you try them and understand how they work, you'll probably find some very useful, practical things you can do with them.

Be curious. Try things. Have fun. It's an approach that's

recommended by respected management gurus such as Tom Peters. It's the philosophy behind some of the most successful businesses today.

Write it down

I had an epiphany this morning in the shower. A great idea for a Daily Motivator column. Later, in my office, I thought maybe I should write it down. But it was such a great concept, that I knew I would remember it when it came time to write the column.

Then things started happening. The phone started ringing. Problems came up and had to be dealt with. I still kept thinking about my idea, and knew it would make a great column. Then, somewhere along the way, I lost it. Perhaps it will come back to me, but I've tried for some time now, re-tracing my steps and thoughts, and I can't seem to bring it back.

I should have written it down. I know better, because that's what I usually do. It's just that this idea was so compelling I thought I'd never lose it. And it made me wonder. How many other things get lost?

It is vitally important to keep a written record of important thoughts and ideas. In today's complex world, with information coming at you all day long, it's just not humanly possible to keep it all in your head. If it's important, write it down!

There's something I notice every time I go back and read material that I wrote years ago. I realize how much I've forgotten, and am thankful I had the foresight to put my ideas in writing.

Make a habit of putting your thoughts in writing. And make a habit of reviewing them on a regular basis. Your mind can only hold so much at once, and it might very well be that the answer you need today is something you thought of months ago. Keeping a written record of your important thoughts and ideas will give you a powerful, effective resource for a life of success.

Winners don't worry about winning

Here's a paradox: those people and businesses that are the most competitive are the ones that don't compete.

Real winners set their own standards, instead of focusing on the competition. They don't care about winning a victory over someone else. Rather, their concern is with doing their absolute best.

When you're winning a race, and you look back, you begin to lose. When you start comparing yourself to your competition, the you allow someone else to set your standards for you. You drop back to their pace. Comparing yourself and your performance to others will only limit you. Don't do it.

In every industry there is a leader. In every group of humans there is a leader. The leaders don't worry about what everyone else is doing. The leaders have their own vision, and because of that they have no competition.

The best way to eliminate your competition is to stop competing. Do your best and stop worrying about the rest.

Attract success like a magnet

Success isn't something that you just go out and get. If you chase it, it will elude you. Instead, you attract success to you by the person you become.

If you want to attract powerful people, you must become powerful. If you want to attract creative people, you must become creative. No one will be attracted to you just because you want something. But when you yourself become impressive, then impressive people will rally around you and be only too willing for you to stand on their shoulders.

The world is full of dreamers who talk big and have impressive plans. No one cares about your dreams, though, unless you back them up with action, discipline and commitment. Actions speak infinitely louder than words.

The greatest thing you can ever offer anyone is the person you've become. If you want the world to give you value and

The Daily Motivator To Go

wealth, then you must become a valuable person. Your most valuable asset is your own personal development. Make yourself competent, attractive, committed, disciplined, skilled.

Become the person you need to be in order to have the life you want. Invest in your future by investing in yourself.

The Sequence of Success

There is only so much time available each day. The choices you make about how that time is used, will determine your situation in life. You create your own future by your actions, and your actions are, ultimately, under your complete control.

So how do you make the right choices? Remember that you have a choice, not only to do something or not to do it, but also WHEN to do it. The sequence in which you take action, is a key component of success.

Successful people do the important things first. Inevitably, when you do the trivial, non-productive things first, there is often no time left to do the important, life-enhancing activities. So learn to focus first on the things that will ultimately make a difference in your life.

The winners in life are people who have the discipline to eat dinner before dessert. Imagine for a moment how you would feel each evening if you ate a big piece of chocolate cake, and a bowl of ice cream, before you had your dinner. Would you then feel like eating a nutritious, well-balanced dinner? Probably not.

Doing the "fun" things first, takes away our appetite for doing the "hard" stuff that really needs to be done if we're to make progress in life. Better to get the important things done first. Then the "fun" is even more enjoyable.

There's nothing wrong with dessert — just remember to eat dinner first.

It pays to listen

I just saw an interesting statistic in Fortune Magazine. A study of top salespeople at large corporations found that the highest performers allowed their customers to do 70% of the talking in a typical sales call.

It pays to listen. Listening is one of the best ways to learn. When you're doing all the talking, you are learning nothing. Just pretending to listen, when you're actually trying to think of what you can say next, is not enough. You must really listen, with the goal of understanding the speaker.

And there is another powerful benefit to listening. It builds tremendous rapport. People love to talk about themselves, their work, their ideas, their opinions. When you listen, and are genuinely interested in what someone else is saying, they will come away from the encounter with a very good impression of you. Listening carefully, and asking questions that convey your sincere interest, will leave a better impression than anything you could possibly say.

Exploit your weakness

It's good to know your strengths, and equally useful to know your weaknesses. For when you're aware of your weaknesses, when you're willing to admit them and face them, you've identified a powerful path for personal growth.

Take a look at yourself. What is holding you back? What is keeping you from living the life you want to live? What part of yourself, is constantly disappointing you? Be honest with yourself. What is your greatest weakness?

When you know your weakness, you know where to put your effort. After all, if you're great with managing your money, but a lousy public speaker, wouldn't it pay you to put your effort into improving your speaking skills, rather than improving your money managing skills?

We have a tendency to want to do the things we're good at. And, indeed, we must make full use of our gifts. But we also must grow. And that means identifying our weaknesses and working on them.

When you look right at your greatest weakness, and decide to do something about it, suddenly it changes from a liability to an asset. Suddenly you have found a way to be highly effective, to make a major difference in your life.

Your weaknesses are lessons waiting to be learned.

Maybe not

Faced with the choice between changing one's mind and proving there is no need to do so, almost everyone gets busy on the proof.
— John Kenneth Galbraith

Do you ever consider that you might be wrong? Do you ever question your assumptions? What's so great about being right, anyway? And what's so terrible about being wrong?

There are many valuable ideas and approaches that are not yours. Unfortunately, to perpetuate your own sense of "being right", you sometimes ignore the perfectly useful perspectives of others. Always "being right" will earn you little more than resentment. It creates barriers and inhibits communication.

Discard the attachment to being right and you'll open up enormous new vistas in your thinking and perception. What if you actually listened to people without trying to figure out how to prove them wrong? Think of what you could learn, of how you could benefit from the experience and perspective of others.

Paradoxically, you'll come closer to the truth when you let go of the need to be right.

Priorities

In order to accomplish anything, you cannot do everything. Life is constantly presenting you with an infinite number of possibilities. Yet no matter how rich, or talented, or well connected you are, you can only do so much. There are only 24 hours in a day.

Everything of value comes at a price. If it didn't have a price, it would have no value. And the price is sacrifice. In order to have anything, you must sacrifice other things. In order to play the violin, you must sacrifice the time it takes to learn and practice the instrument. To take the afternoon off and play golf, you must sacrifice the sale you would have made.

Every time you make a choice, you are expressing your priorities. If you don't like where your life is going, take a good look at your priorities. Not the priorities you claim to have, but the priorities that are revealed by your choices.

Every choice is a decision to sacrifice all the other possibilities. You must decide which possibility is the most important to you at any given time. What are your priorities? Make your choices accordingly.

You can't win 'em all

It is unrealistic to expect that you'll continually achieve one victory after another. There will be disappointments along the way. Success is based on your ability to quickly recover from the losses and move on to the next task.

In anything you attempt, there will be setbacks. Does it make sense to compound the loss by dwelling on it? Of course not. Learn from it, yes — you can almost always learn more from a loss than you can from a victory. And then put it behind you. Move forward with confidence.

When someone says no to you, that's one more step on your path to success. Politely thank them and move on to the next person. When a deal falls through, move on to the next one with increased determination. Even the highest paid professional golfers only win a few of the many tournaments they enter.

No one can win every game. Anyone can be a winner, though, by refusing to be stopped by defeat.

What are you good at?

Whatever you're good at, do it! You have gifts — use them!

The things you do well, are the things you enjoy. They're the things that challenge your creativity. They're the things that motivate you to learn, to experiment, to attempt, to persevere, to grow. They give you satisfaction and a genuine feeling of accomplishment.

Find a way to do what you do well. That doesn't necessarily mean you have to get another job, or start your own business. Rather, incorporate your special gifts into everything you do, wherever you do it, in whatever the context.

You're unique. You have experience that no other person has. You have special talents, skills, and a unique perspective. Other people can benefit from what you have. Look for ways to make a unique contribution, and you'll unleash the power and fulfillment that is already a part of you.

Enjoy the journey

The best players enjoy the game. The best musicians have a love for music. The highest achievers enjoy the achievement. Do you detect a pattern here?

Whatever you must do to achieve success, find a way to enjoy it.

You can either do what you love, or love what you do. It doesn't matter which. What matters is the "do" part. Taking the action is what brings success. Yes, you can struggle against your own desires, be miserable, and eventually accomplish your goal. But why? You'll be far more effective and consistently successful when you enjoy doing the things that bring you success.

Healthy, physically fit people enjoy fruits, vegetables, and regular exercise just as much as overweight, out of shape people enjoy eating pizza in front of the TV. The difference is not in the food or the activity — the difference is attitude.

You're in complete control of what you enjoy, and what you dislike. The things you like, are the things you've conditioned yourself to like. And you have the power to change them.

Keeping Score

The best way to stay competitive is to ignore the competition. Run your own race. When you look back to see who is gaining on you, you lose ground. When you start trying to match your competition blow for blow, product for product, feature for feature, then you're playing their game.

Instead, set your own standards. Why waste time keeping score when you could put that effort into improving your performance? The only way to create value, wealth and abundance in your own life is to provide value to the lives of others. This requires focusing on the "for", rather than the "against."

You'll never be competitive by reacting to someone else's actions, especially in this fast-paced world. Better to put your energy into doing the best that you can possibly do. Competitors try to capture a share of the market. Leaders create their own market. Take your own initiative and excel at your own game.

Get started right away

Once you make the decision, once you set a goal for yourself, start acting on it immediately. That is how momentum is created. Don't move on to anything else until you have committed some action to your goal.

And then follow through. Keep the momentum going by taking consistent action. Your initial determination will get you started, and your discipline to act consistently will get you all the way there.

Don't stop, or it will take that much more effort to get started again. You're already on the way, so keep going. You've invested your time and effort, and your hopes. And the investment will pay off handsomely when you "hold it until maturity" by taking consistent action.

With commitment and perseverance, anything is possible.

Being your best

No one is better than you

You are just as good, just as worthy, just as valuable as anyone. No one can intimidate you, no matter what kind of car they drive, or what their business card says, or how big their house is, or how big their factory is. No one is better than you.

You are the best there is. Inside you is the potential to do, or be, or have anything you desire. No one has more than that. Some may have progressed farther down the path at this moment, but that doesn't make them any better than you.

There is no need for you ever to be envious or to feel unworthy. Your life is filled with possibility. Where you are right now is insignificant, when compared to where you're going. Point yourself in the direction of your dreams, and every step along the way is golden.

No matter what anyone says, or does, no matter what your situation — personal, financial, social or otherwise — you can choose to live your life your own way. And there is no greater success than that.

Look around you — there you are!

Think for a moment about what your environment is like. What makes up the day-to-day "stuff" or your life? Your environment has a powerful influence on your growth and success. If you spend your days surrounded by things that are limiting, your success will be limited. When you spend your time in an environment that is uplifting, it will bring true success to your life.

Take a serious look at your environment...

What kind of food do you eat? Do you fill your body with junk, or with high-energy nutrition?

Do you sit mesmerized for hours in front of the TV? Or do

you seek out new, real-life experiences on a regular basis?

What kind of people do you like to associate with? Are they people who spend time and energy on petty gossip and instant gratification? Or are they people who challenge you to better yourself — physically, intellectually and spiritually?

How are your living spaces — your home, your office, your vehicle, your neighborhood? Are they trashy, cluttered and broken down, or are they clean, organized and well-maintained?

What about your spiritual environment? Are you just drifting through life, or do you have a clear sense of purpose and values.

Every part of your life affects every other part. You can't expect to live in a dysfunctional environment at home and be successful in your career. You can't expect to have any great accomplishments in your life when you spend your evenings bar hopping or channel surfing.

Look at your surroundings — the places, the people, the activities, the values. These things define you. And you have control over them. If you don't like what your environment says about you, then take steps to change it. Start eating better quality food (bananas don't cost any more than potato chips). Hang out with people who challenge and stimulate you, and leave the petty gossip to someone else. Clean up and organize your desk, your car, your home and your yard. Turn off the TV. And take the time develop a clear understanding of your purpose in life.

Build an environment that's suitable for the person you desire to be.

Be different

When those around you are greedy and shallow — be caring and giving.

When those around you are lazy and apathetic — be full of energy and enthusiasm.

The Daily Motivator To Go

When those around you are worried and depressed — be confident.

When those around you are frantic — be calm.

When those around you are stubbornly stuck in their old ways — try something new.

When those around you do mediocre work — do excellent work.

When those around you complain about everything they have — be thankful for everything you have.

Going along with the crowd will cause you to be just one of the crowd, living someone else's dream. What joy is there in that?

Stand up and stand out. Refuse to accept mediocrity. Refuse to accept things just because "that's the way we've always done it." Do what you need to do. Do what is right. Instead of following the well-worn path, blaze a new and exciting trail into unknown territories. The world rewards those who have the confidence and courage to stand out from the rest.

Life is too precious to waste it on silly pretenses. Be and express the unique person you are.

Feeling Good

Look at all the pain and heartache that happens in the pursuit of "feeling good." Drug and alcohol abuse, obesity, infidelity, AIDS — all are rooted to a significant degree by the desire to "feel" good. It's a high price to pay, especially when you realize that (a) When abused, things like food, drugs and sex don't really feel all that good anyway, and (b) nothing outside yourself is really necessary in order to feel good.

You can feel good simply by deciding that you do! You're in complete control of your feelings. You can decide how to react to various situations.

You don't need that cigarette or that package of cookies. You only think you need them because of how you've been conditioned. But you are more powerful than your conditioning or your habits. Your life and your feelings are under your command.

When a problem comes up, instead of reaching for a six-pack to "drown your sorrows" and make you "feel good", try a little re-framing. Look at the problematic situation as an opportunity, and be thankful for the chance to learn and grow. Then feel good about your ability to meet challenges head on.

The best way to feel good is simply to allow yourself to do it.

Looking in the mirror

Do you ever find yourself getting frustrated or angry with the actions of others?

Whatever you see when you evaluate other people, is a projection of what is inside of you. When you find yourself thinking, "I wish she could make a firm decision" it is an indication of your own frustration at not being able to make a decision. In order to recognize something in others, you must first have it within yourself.

Think about it. Is there something that makes you particularly angry? Why? Look inside yourself for the source of this anger. Even if you could change the behavior of others, it would not resolve your own feelings. You are the only one who can change the way you feel. Trying to run away by blaming others, will only prolong the problem and make it worse.

The really good news is, that this "mirror" has a positive side to it. The inspiring, uplifting things you see in other people, are in you as well. When you see in others such things as compassion, genius, beauty, caring and affection, you're seeing a projection of yourself. You're able to see these things because they are a part of you.

The source of your thoughts and feelings about other people, about things, about situations, is you. When you see darkness, it is your darkness. When you see beauty, it is your own beauty. Grasp this concept, and you have the power to change your world.

Like Yourself

The only way you can successfully communicate and relate to other people, is to like yourself. The more you like yourself, the more others will like and accept you. Unfortunately, many people have experiences in their past that leave them feeling unworthy, incapable and embarrassed.

That is all over now. It is in the past. The reality is that you're an expressive, sensitive, gregarious person, if only you'll let yourself be. It doesn't matter what someone has said about you in the past. It doesn't matter what shortcomings you have previously experienced. That is all history.

What matters is what you do from this point forward. Realize that you are a worthwhile, valuable person with an enormous contribution to make. Find the best within yourself and feel good about the person you are. You are a special person, and your life begins today.

You make it special

Think of the moments in your life that have been truly special. Not the times that are built up to be grand and exalted, but rather those experiences which you will carry with you forever.

What was it that made them special? It was whatever you put into them. It was your effort, your commitment, your sacrifice, the part of yourself that you gave to the moment.

The moments of life are as special as you make them. It is what you give that makes your life meaningful. The more you give, the more you are. Your life is defined by the contributions you make, not by the car you drive or the parties you attend.

Great art only happens when the artist puts himself into the work. Great literature comes only when the writer puts herself into the story. A life of excellence requires that you put yourself into the effort.

You're one of a kind

There is no one else, anywhere, who has your own special combination of skills, interests, contacts, knowledge, values and experience. You're the only one there is. You have no competition when it comes to being you.

Anything you can do to more fully develop the unique person you are, will serve you well in all areas of life. What do you love to do? That's probably what you'll be most successful at doing. What things fascinate you and hold your interest? Those are the areas where others will value your perspective and insight. What is it that you MUST do, that you cannot not do? It is there that you will find the passion necessary to overcome any obstacle.

In this interconnected, de-centralized world it is more important than ever to be a unique individual. The opportunities to thrive and prosper by being just a "cog in a wheel" are fast disappearing. They're being replaced by opportunities for people who are creative and resourceful, who can contribute their own unique perspective.

Let yourself be the person you are. That is the very best person you can be.

Look up and smile

The more you look up, the more things will be looking up.

The more positive you are in a physical sense, the more positive your whole life is. Your mind and your body work together. It is difficult to be mentally and spiritually joyful and positive when you have a negative, lifeless physiology.

Conversely, when you are smiling, standing or sitting up straight, looking upward, and breathing deeply, it is almost impossible to sustain negative attitude. Act positive physically and you will be positive. You'll see the good things around

The Daily Motivator To Go

you. You'll interact better with other people.

Think about it, who would you rather deal with, someone who is slumped over and looking down at the ground, or someone who is sincerely cheerful, smiling, bright eyed, looking up, and full of positive energy.

Have you ever looked at someone and known immediately that they were depressed? Of course. It is easy to spot. So, if you don't want to be depressed, don't act depressed. It works every time. If you want to be joyful, act joyfully.

Try it right now. Experience the contrast for yourself. First, look down, slump over, put a scowl on your face, and say "things are terrible." That feels awful, doesn't it? Now, sit up, look upward, put a big smile on your face and say with excitement and passion "this is a great day and I feel fantastic." Notice how much better you feel? It really works.

Sit up straight, throw your shoulders back, take a deep breath, look up — live your life with energy, passion, and joy.

Self interest

It is not from the benevolence of the butcher,
the brewer, or the baker that we expect our dinner,
but from their regard to their own interest.
— Adam Smith

Take care of yourself first. No matter how much you may want to give to others, if you don't have anything yourself, then you have nothing to give.

Self interest is not selfish. It is highly responsible. Taking care of yourself means being responsible for yourself, and there is nothing selfish about that.

Self interest is a powerful creative force. Because she knows she will be rewarded, the scientist works diligently to develop a new medicine. Because he knows he will be rewarded, the investor finances a new venture.

The more you take care of yourself, of your own needs and desires, the more you have to contribute to life. And the more you have to contribute, the more you become. It is an upward spiral that begins when you take responsibility for your own life, and begin to look out for your own interest. Everyone benefits when you take care of yourself.

You're a winner today

Congratulations! You're a winner today. The good things you expect, will come to you. The actions you take, will bring results. The opportunities you look for, will appear.

The people you serve, will give you their support. The effort you put forth, will bring rich rewards. The value you create, will add to your wealth.

The love you give, will bring you joy. The burdens you shoulder, will make you strong. The problems you solve, will make you wise.

The moments you fill with purpose and care, will bring fulfillment. You're a winner today. The good things you do will come back to you.

Problems and opportunities

Life is not fair

"That's not fair" is a favorite expression of young children. "She got a bigger cookie. It's not fair." "He got a purple balloon and I got a red one. It's not fair." I suppose in our attempt to teach our children the concepts of equity and justice, we give them the impression that life is, or should be, fair.

Nothing could be further from the truth. Life is not fair. And furthermore, we wouldn't really want it to be. If it was, then we'd all be exactly the same. Just think how boring that would be. Everyone would have the same kind of car, the same kind of house, the same education, the same income, the same personality, the same physique, the same everything. Who would want that?

Life is not fair because life is what we make of it, and we all choose to live it differently. What is a priority for some, means nothing to others. Life could not possibly be fair unless we all conspired to make it so, and why would we want to do that? The excitement, the challenge, the variety, the essence of life comes precisely from the fact that it is not fair. Some people are born with all the advantages, and others come into life with almost nothing going for them. Is that fair? No. Does it make life worth living? Absolutely.

You have some advantages that others don't have. And others have advantages that you don't have. That's just the way it is. We each have our own burdens and our own joys, from both of which we can learn and grow. When we accept the fact that life is not fair, then we begin to make it great.

It's not what you have, it's what you do with it

In the nineteenth century, before the invention of the internal combustion engine, crude oil was a nuisance. No one wanted it on their property — it fouled the land and the water.

Then came the internal combustion engine, and the automobile, and the petroleum business. Suddenly, there was a huge market for crude oil because someone had figured out something useful to do with it.

Nothing other than life itself really has intrinsic value. In order for anything to have value, you must know what to do with it. And the more productively you can use it, the more value it has.

At the heart of every computer is a microprocessor chip made primarily of silicon. Silicon is more abundant in nature than any other element except for oxygen. As you walk down any beach in the world, the sand beneath your feet is composed largely of silicon. Yet silicon, when processed into a computer chip, can be worth thousands of times its weight in gold. What is it that makes silicon so valuable? It's not the material itself — it's the fact that someone has taken it and purified it and processed it into something extremely useful.

Knowing what to do with something is more important than the thing itself. This holds true not only for tangible, material things but also for things such as ideas, business contacts, skills and information. Most people are caught up in the endless pursuit of trying to get enough, of trying to have enough. Such an approach will never work, because just having enough is never enough. You must know what to do with it. In fact, when you know what to do with what you have, you'll discover that you already have enough.

That is a very powerful concept. It frees you from the dead-end approach of getting, and focuses you on the wealth-creating approach of giving.

The Daily Motivator To Go

What if a manufacturing plant opened up, and all they did was stockpile raw materials? Certainly the raw materials are necessary for productive manufacturing. If nothing is done with them, though, they are virtually worthless. To produce wealth, the people operating the plant need to figure out what to do with all those raw materials, and then they need to do it.

The same holds true for you. In order to produce wealth, you need to figure out what to do with what you've got. How can you produce maximum value for others, using the skills, knowledge, contacts and resources at your disposal? Answer that question, and you'll immediately start creating wealth.

Good Luck!

Have you ever wondered how some people can be lucky enough to be in the right place at the right time?

Well, we're all in the right place at the right time. It's just that some people don't know it, and others are not prepared for it. The folks we call "lucky" are the people who can see opportunity and who are prepared to take advantage of it.

There is always opportunity. Even in the most dismal of times, there are things that need to be done. The people who step forward to do those things are the "lucky" ones who enjoy success. Opportunity is always present, but it is rarely obvious. To be lucky, you must learn to look at a situation and see opportunity where others see nothing. This requires an open mind and what we now refer to as "out-of-the-box" thinking. It requires that you look at situations from many different perspectives, all the time wondering "what if?" It requires a certain amount of detachment, so you can view your situation without being clouded by emotion. It requires the courage to try something completely new and the confidence to follow your own path.

Lucky people are also the ones who are prepared for opportunity. Being prepared primarily requires discipline. Discipline is not easy. It requires that you put out sustained effort over a long period. It takes discipline to learn new skills, to accumulate capital, and to make new contacts. And these are the kinds of things you'll need to take advantage of the opportunities you discover.

Want to be lucky? Open your eyes to the opportunities around you, and discipline yourself to make the most of them.

Frustration

Are you constantly frustrated?

Good!

Tony Robbins tells us that all successful people know "success is buried on the other side of frustration". The only people who are not ever frustrated are those who never attempt anything.

If you're taking action and working toward achievement of your goals, you will become frustrated on a routine basis. People don't follow through on their word, machines break down, projects take longer than you estimated, accidents happen. There are thousands of things that can go wrong.

But that doesn't need to stop you. The best way to deal with frustration is to adjust your attitude. Accept the fact that you'll have setbacks, and look for what you can learn from them. Beating yourself up, because of something over which you have no control, is certainly not productive. Instead, ask yourself, "What can I learn from this?" "How can I make sure this doesn't happen again?"

And you can take the concept one step further. If something is frustrating you, there's a good chance that it's a problem for other people as well. Perhaps if you developed a good solution, it would be valuable to a lot of people. Who knows, you might could even make some money from it. Look at your frustrations as opportunities for improvement.

Resiliency

It's not how many times you get knocked down that counts, it is how fast you can get back up. Everyone who is attempting anything worthwhile, will suffer setbacks. The faster you get past them, the less damage they'll do.

The most frustrating setbacks are those over which you have no control. The best way to bounce back is to find something you CAN control. Find something positive that you CAN do and do it. Get past your frustration by shifting your focus to where you can make a difference. Maintain your momentum by continuing to be effective in some way. Delight in your accomplishments, and realize that you have what it takes to overcome any adversity.

When something has you frustrated because it is beyond your control, take action to ensure that you don't get in that position again. Realize that you can take control of your own life, even if you don't control the situation.

If anything is blocking your path, go around it rather than beating your head against it. Get back up, look clearly at what must be done, and then do it. The game is won by the player who can keep on coming back no matter what.

Getting Past Denial

Many times we make problems worse by not wanting to even admit they exist. It seems easier to simply avoid the problem, rather than face up to it and deal with it. Ultimately, the avoidance becomes more painful than the original problem.

Ironically, the best way to limit life's pain, is to accept that some pain is necessary. Accept that life is full of problems, and that it is through the pain of resolving these problems, that we learn and grow.

Many people live in a constant state of denial, afraid of the pain it would cause to look their situation straight in the eye. Yet, as soon as you get past that denial, your situation has already improved. You're able to see the mistakes you've made in the past, and to learn from your experience. You're able to clearly evaluate your current situation, and construct a workable, realistic plan for your life.

Realize that, though you are responsible for your actions, who you are is not defined by what you have done. Everyone makes mistakes. Detach yourself from your problems, and then look at them realistically, with the goal of solving them.

Life if full of challenges. Have the courage to look at them clearly, and you'll see that they are all opportunities in disguise.

Be prepared for opportunity

Before everything else, getting ready is the secret of success.
— Henry Ford

You must be prepared to answer when opportunity knocks. Because most opportunities won't wait. And the fewer opportunities you take advantage of, the fewer there will be.

Imagine going to visit a friend. He offers you a drink, and you politely say "no, thank you." After a few minutes, he'll repeat his offer. "Are you sure you don't want a drink?" "No, thank you," you say. And he'll probably ask you a third time. If you refuse his offer three times, chances are he won't offer you a drink again that day. You've convinced him that you don't want one.

Life is the same way. When good things come your way, and you ignore them repeatedly, soon they just stop coming at all. You've convinced the world that you don't want what it has to offer. Better to be prepared, because each opportunity you're able to seize will lead to countless other possibilities.

Winners train for months and years before the actual competition. The winning is really in the preparation, not in the race itself. Being prepared will make you strong, bold, confident and competent.

Practice preparation. Be sure you're ready to make the best of all that life has to offer.

You never know...

Think about the incredible series of coincidences that have led you to where you are today. Chances are, there have been many moments, seemingly insignificant at the time, that ended up altering the course of your life in a major way. Perhaps it was someone you met, who introduced you to someone else, through whom you met your spouse. Or perhaps it was a party you attended, and someone you talked to, who knew someone else, who was responsible for your current job.

You never know what will come your way, or how it will come. Things happen in the most unexpected ways. People come into your life, and lead you to other people, who lead you to others, and so on. That person standing in line behind you at the bank might just hold your future in his hands.

That's why it's so important to be open to new ideas, new people, and new experiences. If you sit in front of the TV all the time, life-changing opportunities will rarely come your way. Get yourself out, circulating among people, doing things, exchanging ideas and participating in life. Opportunities come in abundance each day when you are open to them.

Peace and acceptance

Let life flow

Try to hold water in your hand, and it slips away. Immerse yourself in the water, let it flow around you, and you can experience it as long as you wish.

Life is much the same way. Life cannot be contained or held in your hand. To experience life, you must immerse yourself in it. You cannot squirrel it away or keep it only to yourself. You must let life flow through you to fully experience its joy.

It is not necessary to possess in order to enjoy and experience. Too often, we spend so much time and effort trying to hold and possess, that we are unable to enjoy whatever it is we desire. The concept of "need" assumes limitations. When you free yourself from the need to possess, you are free of limitation.

Learn to appreciate and experience beauty, people, food, and ideas without having to own or devour them. It will bring you lasting, unconditional freedom, peace and joy.

Forgiveness

How much time and energy do you spend carrying a grudge? What does it get you? Does it improve your life, or the lives of others?

Forgiveness is very liberating. When you blame others for your troubles, you give them control over your life. Being able to forgive, to let it go, puts you back in control.

Of course you don't want to let people take advantage of you. But if someone has already harmed you or slighted you, there's no need to continue making it worse for yourself by fretting and worrying about it. When someone cuts you off on the freeway, it's a bad experience. Should you make it worse by fuming and complaining about it for the rest of the day?

Take what you can from it, learn from it, and then let it go.

Let it go, and get on with your life. Turning the other cheek benefits you more than anyone else.

Let it go

How do you react when you receive an inflammatory e-mail? What do you do when someone is rude to you?

Are you quick to take offense, anxious to get even, eager to teach the person a lesson? When someone is riding on your bumper in heavy traffic, do you pull over and let them pass, then catch up to them and ride their bumper for a while, just to "let them see how it feels"? I admit that I've done this little routine several times. Then I realized something: this kind of behavior was accomplishing absolutely nothing for me. Over time, I've learned the power of "letting it go."

The admonition in the Bible to "turn the other cheek" is not just a weak and wimpy way out of a situation. It is a powerful strategy that always prevails in the end. If you react to what someone else does, it doesn't matter what your reaction is — that person controls you. In fact, the weak response is to lash out at someone. The strong response is to continue on the path you set for yourself, rather than be deterred by the actions of someone else.

This is not to say that you should sit back and take abuse from others. If someone has it in for you, by all means get out of the way. Don't waste a lot of time plotting revenge, though. It is an enormous waste.

Think for a moment. What good is it going to do you to get all upset about someone who cuts you off on the freeway? When something like this happens, you actually have a choice. You can either let it consume you, and set a negative tone for the whole day, or you can let it go, and move on to more important concerns.

Closely related to reaction is blame. Blame is a trap that many people fall into. Trying to assign and publicize blame for situations and events is fruitless. It really doesn't matter who is to blame, because there's nothing you can do about it. Knowing who to blame does not change the situation. Don't waste your time figuring out who is responsible for a bad situation. Instead, spend your efforts to determine who is best equipped to get you out of the situation.

Taking offense and dwelling on blame get you high blood pressure, wasted time, lots of enemies, and negative energy. Forgiving and forgetting get you peace of mind, friends, and a positive outlook, not to mention more time available for productive pursuits.

Challenge yourself today to try and let things go. Watch your reactions, and don't let people or situations exert their control over you. Know your own path, and follow it confidently. That will make it difficult for anyone to dislodge you from it.

Acceptance

Things are the way they are. You are the person you are. You life is the way it is. You can either accept these things, or make yourself miserable about them.

There are no doubt many things you think you should have done, and many other things you wish you had not done. Accept these things. You cannot change them by pretending they did or didn't happen.

Take a deep breath. Relax. Accept the person you are. Accept the people and the world around you.

Acceptance doesn't mean being passive. If there's something you want to change, then take action to change it. Acceptance doesn't mean that you approve of or support something. It just means that you see it for what it is. That you don't deceive yourself about it.

Acceptance will help you to see clearly, to learn and to grow. Think of a baby learning to walk. When he stumbles and falls, he doesn't get depressed, or paranoid, or embarrassed, or angry. He doesn't develop a guilt complex, or ulcers, or high blood pressure. He doesn't try to pretend like the fall didn't happen. He simply pulls himself up on the nearest supporting object. He enthusiastically tries again, accepting the fact that he'll have to fall many times before learning to walk. In an environment of acceptance, true learning and growth take place.

Bring peace, patience, learning and accomplishment to your life by practicing acceptance.

Boredom

Are you ever bored?

In this hurry-up world, our days are frequently scheduled and structured with business and personal matters that need attention. There is often too little time for quiet, unstructured boredom. And with television, the Internet and other information media constantly bombarding us, there's always something to provide diversion.

We need a little boredom, though. Time that is not scheduled or filled with activity. Time to sit and think, to reflect, to relax, to contemplate, to find a little balance. We need quiet time that is not interrupted by a telephone, a newspaper, television, radio or any other distraction.

When was the last time you just let your mind wander, while staring at the clouds? You can learn a lot from times like that. You take in so much on a daily basis, and time is needed to process it all. The problem is, there's so much more constantly coming in, that the processing part gets way behind.

If excitement and activity are all you know, then they cease to be special and just become tedious. Don't forget to balance them with some quiet, thoughtful boredom on a regular basis.

Patience

A sense of urgency is crucial to success, and yet just as important to success is patience. These may seem at first to be contradictory attributes, but really they are not. For we must

172

learn to act with urgency, and react with patience. Yes, we reap what we sow — sow with a sense of urgency, and reap with a rational patience.

We must have the patience to let our efforts bear fruit. Nothing worth having can be created immediately. There will be delays, disappointments and setbacks. Patience will help you put it all into perspective, and will give you the perseverance necessary to reach your goals.

Patience will make you confident and decisive. Patience will help you to avoid stress. Patience will give you a rational outlook that eventually leads to success. It will help you to become disciplined, and to avoid poor decisions made in haste.

The keys to patience are acceptance and faith. Accept things as they are, and look realistically at the world around you. Have faith in yourself and in the direction you have chosen.

Learn to be patient and savor the richness of your life.

Balance

Life could not exist without a constantly maintained balance. Just as your physical self requires chemical and mechanical balance, successful living demands balance on many levels.

Work like it matters, and live like it doesn't. Do your best, and accept your worst. Enjoy the beauty that is, and never let it make you complacent. Visualize your dreams so that they are real enough to touch, and recognize the reality of the effort needed to achieve them.

Let your mind wander openly, and keep your efforts focused. Carefully consider your options, and take decisive action. Work hard, and relax completely. Take risks, and protect yourself from threats. Be compassionate, and be challenging. Love, and be wary. Be enthusiastic, and be discreet.

Give praise, and offer useful criticism. Be outrageous, and always disciplined. Live free, and practice moderation. Enjoy the material world, and let your spirit soar without limit.

Relax under pressure

Imagine yourself in a difficult situation with your boss, your spouse, your child, an irate customer. The other person is very angry and tense, and you are the target of their anger. How do you react? Do you meet fire with fire, become defensive, raise your voice? Does that really accomplish anything?

Have you ever thought of consciously trying to relax when the world around you is tense, upset or irritated? When the pressure is really on, you can dramatically improve your own performance by remaining calm and relaxed.

Impossible? No, not at all. You always have complete control over your emotions, your actions. You can choose to be angry and tense, or you can choose to be relaxed. Realize that your reaction is just that, a reaction. You are not under the control of the other person.

Say to yourself, "I am going to take a deep breath, relax my shoulders, my neck, my back, and meet this situation with calmness. Rather than giving the power over my thoughts to this other person, I will keep control of my own thoughts and work to resolve this situation."

Even when the anger and tension is not specifically directed at you, an attitude of calm relaxation and control can help you to make the best of any situation.

Let it be, and make it happen

Better to work for than to fight against. Better to create your own market, than to go against the competition. Better to promote your own cause, than to fight against another cause.

When you fight against something, even if you win, you only break even — and strengthen the resolve of your opponent.

Some fights are necessary. When you're attacked you often have no choice. Yet fighting will rarely get you ahead. The biggest winners transcend the fight, and make their own way unopposed. The best athletes barely notice their opponents. The most successful companies focus on excellence, rather than on the competition. The winner of the race never looks back.

When you have a choice, choose not to fight. Rather, find a way to make your own rules. Defeat your opponents by ignoring them as you make your way to the top.

Peace

Rarely in today's world do we ever take time to enjoy a few peaceful moments. In the interconnected, Internet-driven business world, it is always "business hours" somewhere. And even when we're not doing business, we're busy entertaining or being entertained, socializing, exercising, eating, playing, sleeping, shopping, cleaning, gardening or keeping all of our stuff maintained.

When was the last time you spent a quiet moment just doing nothing — just sitting and looking at the sea, or watching the wind blowing the tree limbs, or waves rippling on a pond, a flickering candle or children playing in the park? When was the last time you didn't have something scheduled, that you could just relax and sit until you were ready to move on?

Sometimes we need time to sort things out. Especially in the hurry-up world where information comes at us with blazing speed. A few peaceful moments now and then can help us to see more clearly, to put things in perspective. There is so much beauty around us, in the things we hurry past every day. Beauty that can, if we let it, spark our creativity, provide balance, give us strength and inspire us. It is important to have a time when we let down our defenses, just accepting and enjoying the beauty around us.

Stop every now and then. Just stop and enjoy. Take a deep breath. Relax and take in the abundance of life.

The Daily Motivator To Go

Wealth and abundance

Focus on Abundance

Your mind is a powerful force. It is your most able servant, and it will produce for you whatever you focus it on. If you are constantly focused on scarcity — worrying about not having enough money — then your mind will create even more scarcity.

On the other hand, when you constantly think about abundance, and focus your thoughts on the gifts you already have and how you can make the best use of them, then your mind will help to create abundance for you. When you look at life as prosperous, it will be prosperous.

Nothing that's external to yourself has the power to make you happy or unhappy. Your happiness depends on how you choose to feel about the situation you are in. Don't fall into the trap of delaying your happiness by thinking "If I could only have _____, then I'll be happy." That kind of thinking will always deny you the abundance and happiness you seek.

The things in your life are here to serve you — you are not here to serve them. The fear of not having enough will prevent you from seeing that you already are enough. The secret is to stop focusing on what you do not have, and shift your consciousness to an appreciation for everything you are and everything you do have.

Think about what you are worth. Not on a bank statement, but as a person. Think of all the possibilities open to you as a living, thinking human being. You are capable of greatness. Your worth is infinite.

What do you think you deserve? If you feel that you don't deserve to be happy, then you won't be. If you feel you deserve to take what you want at the expense of others, then that will also prevent you from experiencing abundance. You deserve ultimate happiness, and so does everyone else. And it is in the process of helping others, that you serve yourself and all others as well. Imagine for a moment that you possessed everything you could ever possibly want — all the real estate, all the jewels, all the gold, all the luxury cars, homes, boats, planes — anything and everything you wanted! Imagine that it was all at your disposal. Now imagine how it would be, owning all of this stuff, if there was not a single other person alive in the world. Not much point to it all, is there?

When you have a sincere desire to serve others, rather than to serve the "things" you think you want, then your abundance and prosperity will be unlimited.

Creating Wealth

So many people get hung up on trying to "get money." That is not the way to wealth. First of all, you don't just "get" money. You exchange something of value for money, if you want money. Money, however, is not what anyone wants. What we want are the things that we can exchange the money for.

The way to wealth is to create something valuable that has not ever existed before. This can be tangible or intangible, it doesn't really matter. All that matters is that it is valuable. What do I mean by valuable? I mean that it is valued by other people who are willing to exchange their own things of value in order to receive the benefits of what you have created.

You can create a product, a place, a concept, a work or art, a network of people, whatever. Most likely your creation will be a combination of things. And creation does not necessarily imply "creativity" in the sense that we normally think of it. Building something is creating, even if you're not the one who originally thought of it.

The point is, you cannot "get" rich, unless you are lucky enough to receive an inheritance or win the lottery. To create wealth, you must create value. One of the very best ways to create value is to solve problems. The world is full of opportunities to create value and wealth — and these opportunities come disguised as problems.

Look around you. Opportunity is everywhere. There is plenty of abundant wealth just waiting to be created.

You're worth whatever you think you're worth

It has been shown in studies that it's almost impossible for people to earn 5% more than what they think they're worth. And by the same token, it is almost impossible for people to earn 5% less than what they think they're worth. Apart from qualifications, experience and market conditions, someone who earns $20,000 a year will usually find another job earning about $20,000 a year. And someone who earns $250,000 a year will usually be able to find another job earning $250,000 a year.

The only way this changes is when you change your expectations of yourself, and the value you place on yourself. If you see yourself earning minimum wage, then you'll earn minimum wage. If you see yourself earning $100,000 a year, that's what you'll earn.

No matter what kind of great opportunities are presented to you, if you see yourself as an hourly worker, if don't believe that you deserve success, then something will kick in that will deny success to you.

How do you change your self image, so that you can truly see yourself as successful and prosperous? First, you need to be clearly focused on where you are going, on what you want to accomplish. Determine not only what you want to accomplish, but also why. When you understand why you want success, you'll find a way to get it. You'll do whatever it takes. The why is critical.

Actions are vital, as well. It's not enough to be positive and to be focused. These are important, but it is action that gets you where you want to go. In fact, it is action with which you convince yourself of your sincerity and desire. In the end, only you really know if you're sincerely working in the direction of your goals. Only you know if you're doing your best. Your focus, your desire, and your sense of self worth are powerful tools. And they are fueled by actions. If you want to improve your self worth, then do something worthwhile. Over and over again. Get in the habit of providing value to others, and you'll convince yourself of your own value.

Whatever you want to accomplish, whatever you want to be, must first exist in your mind. You must see yourself as a success in order to become a success. You must value yourself enough that you spend your time doing valuable and worthwhile things. You must value yourself enough to take action, again and again.

Give it up, and have it all

Give up the illusion that you can get something for nothing. It is impossible. Give up looking for a way to bend the rules. You cannot help but cheat yourself. Give up looking for a shortcut or an instant windfall. You get only what you give. Taking the "easy way out" only gets you... out.

Take a deep breath and decide to start living, to start giving, to start making a difference. Realize that your effort and your creativity are what make you alive. Seeking fulfillment through taking and possessing is an empty pursuit that leaves you hungry and desperate. Put your efforts into doing and becoming, instead of wasting your energy with jealously and empty wishes.

Look not at what you can have. Think of what you can do. Think of the life you can create. Think of what you can become.

Give up the need to get, and you can have it all. Give up the need to possess, and the abundance of life is yours to enjoy.

It's not what you need that counts

"I need to lose weight. I need more money. I need to spend more time with my family. I need a better job. I need to win the lottery. I need to finish that project. I need this. I need that."

We hear people saying these things all the time. Everyone's telling us what they need.

Guess what? No one cares what you need. It doesn't matter what you need. Your need is not a sufficient reason for anyone to do anything for you or give anything to you. It's really not. Your need doesn't accomplish anything. It doesn't provide value. What you need doesn't matter.

Some people devote a lifetime to needing. It gets them nowhere. We've recently witnessed the failure of communism as an economic system. The principle of "to each according to his need" is one that is doomed. No society can thrive for very long on such an assumption.

Not that we shouldn't be compassionate. But our compassion should be directed, not at fostering and encouraging need, but at encouraging challenge and effort. If you give a man a fish, you feed him for a day. If you teach him how to catch fish, you feed him for a lifetime.

Which of the following statements do you find to be more powerful?

I really, really need to lose weight.

- or -

I'm committed to doing whatever it takes to lose 10 pounds this month.

It is not what you need that counts. It is what you do. You won't get anything by simply needing it. Value and wealth and all the good things in life are created by effort. Express your goals in terms of desire and action. "I'm taking new steps every day to increase my earning." And then take those actions. Don't dwell on what you need, concentrate on what you can do. Get out of the dead-end "I need" mentality. And just do it.

The journey is the reward

Give two children a room full of toys and they'll soon be fighting over them. Give them a room full of nothing, and they'll soon be cooperating and inventing games to play together.

The high-tech startup company is an exciting place to work. They can barely make the payroll each week, and most of the employees take stock options in lieu of a higher salary. Still, everyone gives it their all, working as a team to get the company established. Then the products begin to succeed in the marketplace. A public offering brings in cash and makes everyone a millionaire. The partners start quarreling. It seems like everyone is getting a divorce. Employees update their resumes. Once the money starts to flow, everything seems to fall apart.

"Be careful what you ask for," the saying goes, "because you might just get it."

Why is it that, so often, when we get what we're after it seems so empty? Because we fail to realize that the journey is the reward. Goals and aspirations are important because of what you become in getting there. Once the goal is reached, it has little value and it's time to set a new goal. Life is a continuous growth process. If you're not growing, you're not living.

There's plenty for everyone

The way to true abundance is to reject the mentality of scarcity.

Stop dwelling on what you DON'T have. Instead, focus on what you COULD have, what you could BE. It makes all the difference in the world. Trying to get what you want by taking it from others will never work. Whether your actions are legal or not, you'll always come up short. Because this "zero-sum" mentality presumes scarcity. And when you dwell on scarcity, that's what you'll get in your life.

Learn to think with an "abundance" mentality. You can start by being thankful for the things you do have. Learn to appreciate the beauty around you. Realize that it's not necessary to own or control the sunset, or the sky, or another person, in order for them to fill your life with joy. Understand that you can have lasting success only by providing value and service to others. The more abundance you provide, the more people you provide it to, the more you yourself will have.

Be really rich

We all need each other.

What would happen to the richest person in the world, if no one else had any money? In such a case, even the greatest wealth would be meaningless.

Abundance cannot be stolen or hoarded. It must be lived.

Too often we see wealth as the result of a "getting" process. We waste an enormous amount of time figuring out how we can "get" this or "get" that. In reality, wealth results from a "creation" process.

And creation means giving of yourself. You have something within you that is valuable and unique. Something that you can use to create all the wealth you could ever need or want. Perhaps it is your fascination with sports, perhaps it is your skill with programming computers, or your ability to bring people together, or your knack for selecting appropriate colors. Maybe it is your extensive network or contacts, or your dedication to physical fitness, or your ability to compose music, or your skill at repairing machinery. It's probably a combination of things, and almost certainly something you enjoy. We find satisfaction in things we were meant to do.

Stop thinking about "getting" and "taking." Start thinking about "producing" and "creating". Within any situation, there are opportunities to make a positive, valuable contribution.

When you're primarily concerned with "What can I do for myself?" you might be able to make a good living. Ask "What can I do for others?" and you're on your way to building a fortune.

The freedom of detachment

Most of us are imprisoned by our attachments: to material things, to other people, to our pride, to money, to the past. Many of the actions we take every day are in an attempt to hold on to things we think we need.

True freedom comes when we learn to discard our need for ownership, when we realize that we don't need to own things or people in order to value and enjoy them.

When you try to hold water in your hand, it will drain away and you'll lose it. Immerse yourself in the water, never trying to hold on to it, letting it flow past you, and you can experience as much of it as you want.

Don't need what you have — have what you need.

If always you think in terms of needing what you have, then you will never have enough. Instead, think in terms of having what you need and you will always enjoy abundance.

You want what?

The difference between want and have is do.

Everyone has great dreams, wonderful plans, incredible intentions. Yet far too few people ever follow up on them. And it's not always because of a lack of desire, or even a lack of action.

What's usually missing is continued, focused, effective effort.

You've got to be clear on what you seek. You must plan precisely how it is to be accomplished. And you must be willing to do whatever is necessary, and to work effectively for as long as it takes, until the goal is reached.

Vague generalities are worthless. Commitment to a specific target and plan of action, is essential.

Working effectively toward a well-defined goal is no more

184   *The Daily Motivator To Go*

difficult than spinning your wheels chasing nebulous dreams. Give clarity to your desires and you'll create the energy needed their fulfillment.

Look how far you've come

Take time today to be thankful for all the good things in your life. Think of everything you've got going for you, the people who care about you, the experiences you've had, your skills and interests, your faith, the beauty of life itself.

The things you appreciate, value, and care for, will increase in your life. Abundance begins with gratitude. Being sincerely thankful for what you already have, will propel you, spiritually, mentally and physically, toward whatever you would like to have.

You know you can do it, because you've already done it. You have filled your life with abundance. Anything you want is within reach, when you appreciate how far you've already come.

Taking action

If only . . .

If only I could win the lottery. If only I could get a new job. If only I could find a husband. If only I could get new carpet. If only I could save some money. If only I could lose some weight. If only my bills were paid. If only my family would understand.

Life is full of "if onlys". They greet us each day, and tuck us into bed at night. They flavor every decision we make. They fill us with regret and frustration. Worst of all, they completely mislead us and give us permission to NOT live up to our potential.

"If only" is a great excuse, especially if it's something totally out of your control. "If only the economy wasn't so bad." There's not much we can do about that one, and so it's easy to blame for all our problems.

"If only" keeps us out of life. "If only I had a better dress to wear, I could go to the party." Right, Cinderella? "If only" keeps us waiting on the sidelines of life.

Do you want to ever get anywhere in life? Then forget about "if only". Stop making excuses and start making progress. Is there something that's holding you back? Then get it out of your way.

Whatever it is, put it out of your mind. Free yourself from the hold of "if only" and allow yourself to transcend your limitations.

Do it NOW

A great freedom comes when you have done everything that needs to be done. When you don't have the burden of things you've said you'd do "later", you are free to pursue your dreams.

The Daily Motivator To Go

When something needs to be done, do it now. Then you only have to deal with it once. If you keep putting it off, you spend an enormous amount of energy worrying about it and feeling guilty about it. And it's still not done. Who needs that? Either do it now, schedule a specific time to do it, or decide not to do it. Don't carry around a lot of vague "laters". They clog your brain and your spirit, and slow you down.

When you stop stockpiling "laters" and start taking decisive action, you gain clarity, focus and effectiveness. Do it now!

Get started

You've been planning the journey for a long time. It will take you to a place where you have always dreamed of going. You have committed yourself to getting there, and can already visualize reaching your destination. You have prepared yourself well for the journey ahead, gathering the resources and developing the skills that you'll need along the way. Now, there's just one thing left to do.

Get started. And then keep going.

Put one foot in front of the other. Then do it again, and again until you get to where you are going. Take action, do what needs to be done. Do it consistently and repeatedly. Do it for as long as it takes.

The planning, the preparation, the commitment, and the right attitude are absolutely essential. And so is the action. The courage and discipline to act on your dreams, will make them a reality. There is no other way.

Will it be uncomfortable? Yes. Comfort accomplishes nothing. Will it be difficult? Absolutely. Anything worthwhile requires real effort.

There is nothing that can equal the satisfaction of accomplishment. Of using your mind and your hands, and your sheer will, to create something that has never existed before. It will happen when you act on your dreams, step by step, day by day, again and again until the job is done.

Plan and do

Great achievements rarely ever come in a single shot. They come from a lot of little steps, one after the other, day after day. The successful people in life are able to visualize their goals, but that's really the easy part. Successful people are also able to visualize the pathway to their goals, the series of steps along the way.

That is why planning is so important. You must learn to plan each day, each week, each month, if you're going to reach the ultimate goal. Great things do not happen by chance. Achievement is not haphazard. You need a strategy, a plan of action. You need to realize that every day is a step along the way, and to plan each day accordingly.

We're all given the same 24 hours in every day, the same 7 days in every week, the same 30 or so days in every month. What we make of that time is largely dependent upon how well we plan and organize the minutes and hours of our lives. Everything you do will have consequences down the road. You can't escape that fact. What you can do is to make sure your actions today will lead to the consequences that you desire.

Visualize the unbroken chain of days stretching into your future. Are all the links there, or does your chain just have a beginning (now) and an ending (where you want to be "someday")? If you see your goals occurring "someday" rather than on some specific day, that "someday" might never come. Seeing the end of the road is a step in the right direction. Now you've got to fill in the middle of the road. What are the steps that will take you to where you want to be?

One useful method is to start with your goal and work backwards. Say you want to sail around the world. To do that you'll need a boat and plenty of experience sailing it. To get the boat you'll need money. To get the experience you'll need to take training courses and crew on other people's boats. To get the money you'll need to save and invest on a monthly basis. To take the training courses you'll need to do some re-

188   *The Daily Motivator To Go*

search and see who offers the best ones. And so on. . .

Any thing you want to do, any goal you have, can be worked backward like this, all the way back to today. Once you work it back all the way, you have a clear picture of what you need to do today, tomorrow, and every day until your goal is realized.

Achievement does not come from wishful thinking. It comes from action. Before you can take action, you need to know what that action is. Look at where you want to be, and lay out the path to get there. Then, when you get started every morning, you'll know exactly where you're going.

The Learning Curve

That which we persist in doing
becomes easier for us to do; not that the nature
of the thing itself is changed, but that our power
to do is increased.

— Ralph Waldo Emerson

Just about everything new that you attempt is difficult at first. You've never done it before, so you don't know what to expect. You don't know how much time things will take. You don't know where to go for information. You're not sure you can do it.

The best approach is to jump right in and try. If there's something you want to, or need to do, then just get started. Take the first step. That first step may be awkward and slow, but you learn from it.

Experience is the best teacher. Sure, you can prepare by reading and watching and analyzing. Don't develop analysis paralysis, though. Don't spend so much time preparing for something, that you never get around to doing it. At some point, you just need to get started. Once you've done that, once you've made that commitment, you have momentum on your side.

And your experience will teach you things that no book ever could.

Addicted to success

Addiction can work against you, or it can work for you. It just depends on what you're addicted to. When you get yourself addicted to success, you'll want more. You'll do whatever it takes to get it.

Look at how many people are addicted to cigarette smoking. It is a smelly, disgusting habit. It's expensive, unhealthy and alienates other people. Yet millions continue to do it. They are unwilling to stop themselves. Why? Because it makes them feel good. Or how about heroin? This addiction is on the rise again. Using heroin requires involvement in an underground culture. It is expensive, it involves sticking a needle into one's own body, and it consumes and destroys life. Yet more and more people are doing it. Why?

Because it feels good.

Success can feel good, too. It can feel very good. And unlike tobacco or heroin, the "high" from success and accomplishment doesn't fade in a matter of hours.

Once you've had a small success, then it becomes easier to get addicted to success. The "high" of accomplishment makes you want more. That's why it is important to set some small, quickly attainable goals. When these goals are reached, you "feel good" and you look for ways to do it again. That's how most addictions start out — small. Each time you experience success, savor it. Enjoy it. This is vitally important, because the more you "feel good", the more addicted you'll be.

Get yourself addicted to success, and you can't help but succeed. Start small, and really savor each accomplishment. You'll be "hooked" in no time. Because it feels so good, you won't want to stop.

Go out and make a lot of mistakes

If you're not making mistakes, you're not doing anything. Action is the only way to accomplish anything, and taking action will bring mistakes.

190   *The Daily Motivator To Go*

So often we try to hide our mistakes, and deny them even to ourselves. Instead, we should take pride in the fact that we're out there trying. There is no better learning experience than making a mistake — that is, if you're willing to admit that you've done so. When you acknowledge your mistakes, you have a better understanding of how to proceed. After all, you have firsthand experience with what doesn't work. That's valuable and useful knowledge.

All successful people constantly review their past actions and look for ways to improve on them. Imagine that — they're anxious to find mistakes even in situations that are generally considered to be successful. Does that tell you something about the value of mistakes as a learning experience?

As you continue to take action, and to learn from the results of those actions, you develop a working knowledge of how to be effective. With this knowledge you can become whatever you want to be.

Effort

The heights by great men
reached and kept
Were not attained
by sudden flight,
But they,
while their companions slept,
Were toiling upward
in the night.

— Henry Wadsworth Longfellow

There is opportunity everywhere. And in order to take advantage of opportunity, you must be prepared. That means "paying your dues."

Nothing is more frustrating than to see an opportunity come along, and not be in a position to benefit from it. It pays to be prepared, and that comes down to plain, hard work. It's not usually glamorous. It's not always exciting. It's not always fun.

It is, however, always necessary.

The Olympic athlete makes it look so effortless, but remember — he has been practicing for years. The business professional seems to have the Midas touch, but she spent years in the field and on the road, learning every detail of her business.

Anyone can have a great idea. Without effort and action, that's all it is — a great idea. It's often easy to spot an opportunity, but even the best opportunity demands preparation, effort and commitment, to come to fruition.

The more you work, the luckier you will become.

Perfection

One of the biggest reasons that things never get done is the desire for perfection. We feel that we have to do something perfectly the very first time. If we don't think that's possible (and it rarely is) then we avoid doing it altogether.

In reality, the only way to even approach perfection is through practice and experience. Highly successful musicians, professional golfers, public speakers, surgeons and others who have mastered a particular discipline, know the value of experience. And experience consists largely of past mistakes. Mistakes are excellent teachers. They're nothing to be afraid of.

Of course anything worth doing is worth doing right. There's nothing wrong with having mastery as your goal. But if you're ever going to get anything done, you must start somewhere. If it's not perfect, so what? Give it your best shot and learn from the experience. If you could do everything perfect the first time, how would you ever learn anything? Learn and live by doing, not by wishing for perfection.

Do it anyway

Do you feel like you don't deserve success? Are you afraid that you might fail? Are you afraid you might succeed? Do you worry what other people would think if you were to enthusiastically follow your dream?

Do it anyway!

Wouldn't it be more comfortable to sit home in front of the TV? What makes you think you could possibly make it? It's never been done before. We've tried that and it didn't work. The odds are against you.

Do it anyway!

For everything that has ever been achieved, there were plenty of reasons not to do it. Plenty of excuses for those who were unwilling to attempt it. Plenty of risk, discomfort, sacrifice and hard work involved.

Achievers know that excuses are worthless. That risk is a part of life. That with enough commitment, a well-developed plan, and hard work — anything is possible. Achievers take action while others debate the merits and perfect their excuses.

When you have a dream, follow it. When you see an opportunity, act on it. You DO deserve it, you CAN do it, it WILL take effort and sacrifice. You'll make mistakes and you'll learn from them. You'll have successes and you'll build on them. Take action toward your dream and you'll never have cause for regret.

Excuse busters

For everything that needs to be done, there are always dozens of excuses for not doing it. Doubt and fear will paralyze you if you let them. Resolve to bust your excuses by turning them on their head. Your goals, your dreams are too important to be stopped by lame excuses. The next time you feel an excuse coming on, fight back with this list of excuse busters.

I don't know how — Then make the effort to learn.

It's too hard — Anything worth having, or doing, or being, requires effort.

It will take too long — Then that's all the more reason to get started right away.

What will people think — That's their problem. Let them think what they will. It doesn't matter.

I'll do it as soon as I get back on my feet — Taking positive action toward your goals is precisely what will GET you back on your feet.

I might fail — Yes, when you try you might fail. However, if you don't try, then you'll certainly fail.

I'm too busy — What are you accomplishing with all that busy-ness? Simply being "busy" gets you nowhere. Stop being busy, evaluate your priorities, and start taking focused, directed action.

I don't know where to start — Envision the ultimate goal, and work backwards, step by step, until you arrive at something that can be done right now. Then do it. "The journey of a thousand miles begins with a single step." Take that step, and then the next one. Repeat until done.

I have too many obligations — In order to be of service to others, you must first be true to your own purpose in life. Your obligation to yourself is what enables you to fulfill your obligations to others.

These things never work out — That is correct. "Things" never do work out. You must work them out. The various situations you encounter provide you with opportunities, not sure bets. You must recognize those opportunities and do the work necessary to take advantage of them.

You deserve the best from yourself — no excuses. Spend your energy taking action, rather than thinking up excuses.

Get to work

Things are never as difficult as they seem, once you get started. Just put one foot in front of the other. Just take the first sheet of paper off the top of the stack, and go to work. Dig in and keep going. Make yourself comfortable. Feel the sense of satisfaction and accomplishment as you get things done.

No matter what you do, give it your full attention and do your best. Don't worry about making it perfect. Do make it valuable and useful. Enjoy and appreciate your work. Take pride in it.

The work you do, whatever it is, is an opportunity. An opportunity for your to express the very special person that you are. An opportunity for you to make a difference. An opportunity for you to enrich your own life and the lives of those around you.

Trying and doing

"I'm trying to finish that report."

"Let's try to get together."

"I'm going to try to lose weight."

"He's trying to make ends meet."

Trying is not enough. Doing is the only thing that counts. In fact, trying can be worse than doing nothing at all. When you are "trying" to do something, you're under the illusion that you're actually doing something, and so you don't make any effort to do any more.

Trying is action without commitment. You might try today, yet there's no guarantee that it will continue tomorrow. On the other hand, doing something means that you're committed to taking action until you have accomplished it.

So what's the real difference between "trying hard" to do something, and actually doing it? Nothing, and everything. It's all in your attitude. To all outward appearances, trying is the same as doing. The big difference is inside. The big difference is — how committed are you to getting it done?

Trying wastes a lot of time. When you're not committed to getting it done, you lack focus and effectiveness. Accomplishment comes through doing. When you make the commitment to do whatever it takes, you bring into focus the energy needed to succeed.

"I'm trying to put a book together" or "I'm writing a book." Which book will people be reading soon?

Trying will get you trials. Doing will get you results. Stop trying. Start doing.

Hope

Hope is a good breakfast,
but it is a bad supper.
— Francis Bacon

We must live WITH hope, yet we cannot live BY hope. It is fine to hope for the best. That, however, is not enough. We cannot merely hope, we must take action.

It is sad how many things are tolerated in the hope that they will improve. Hoping for the best won't do anything. Working and taking action, with hope in your heart, will bring about results. That's a powerful combination. Hope works in your favor only as long as it is accompanied by action and commitment.

Hope cannot replace action. Do what needs to be done, hope or no hope. Hope for the best, and do everything in your power to make it happen. Yes, there is hope. Things will get better — when you make them better.

Start each day with hope, and then get busy working. Let your hope inspire you, rather than console you. Hope for the best, and then do whatever it takes. Hope depends on you.

Planting seeds

When you plant a seed in fertile ground, and water it, and make sure it gets enough warmth and sunshine, it will grow and bear fruit.

It doesn't matter how old you are. It doesn't matter what color your skin is, or how much education you have had. It doesn't matter how many seeds you have planted in the past. It doesn't matter how many books you've read about planting seeds.

The Daily Motivator To Go

What matters is that you plant the seed, and you do what is necessary to make it grow.

Likewise, when you take the actions necessary for success, in whatever endeavor you choose, you will succeed. There is no substitute for action, and there is no stopping the result when you take the necessary action.

What are you waiting for?

What's the use if there's no use?

What good is anything if you don't use it?

What good are your skills and abilities, if you don't make the most of them? What good is being a parent if you never have time for your children? What good is having the latest technical wizardry if you don't learn how to operate it?

What good is life if you don't live it? What good is knowledge if you don't apply it. What good is experience if you don't learn from it? What good is food if you don't eat it. What good is wealth if you hoard it?

Possession has value, only when it has purpose. The only way to benefit from what you have, is to use it. Fulfillment comes not from how much you accumulate, but rather from how much you do, and build, and create and contribute.

You have always had riches beyond measure. Live your abundance by putting it to use. Do all you can with the good things you have.

The pain of not taking action

The two most powerful motivators are the desire to have pleasure and the desire to avoid pain. Of these two, the desire to avoid pain is usually strongest. Normally, we will do more to avoid pain than we will do to seek pleasure.

Is there something you know you need to do, that you have not done? Chances are, the reason you haven't done it is because there is some kind of pain associated with it. Even though taking action could eventually bring you much pleasure, your desire to avoid pain is even stronger than your desire for pleasure. It prevents you from doing what needs to be done.

So how do you get around this? Instead of focusing on the pain of doing it, focus on the pain of NOT doing it. It is painful to quit smoking, or start an exercise program, or make cold calls, or learn a new skill, or to do anything that will improve your life. And yet it is even MORE painful to not do these things. Focus on that bigger, long term pain and it will motivate you to act.

The desire to avoid pain has a powerful effect on your life. Learn to control it instead of letting it control you. Remind yourself that the biggest pain is the pain of regret for not taking action.

Get in the game

Whatever you do not attempt, you will most certainly not achieve. The more you just sit and watch life go by, the less it will be to your liking.

Jump in and make a difference. Your complaints and excuses may be elaborate and well reasoned, yet they give you no fulfillment. If you're not satisfied with the way things are, take action. Only you can fulfill the promise of your own life.

Get in the game, and play it like your life depends on it, because it does. Don't expect it to be easy. The beauty of success and accomplishment are that they're NOT easy. A body builder does not build large muscles by lifting small weights. The challenges are what will make you grow.

Achievement is not what you get. It is what you become. Stand up, step forward, and meet life head on.

Lots of little steps

Few people are able to take giant steps — to become an overnight phenomenon. It happens, but it is rare. Yet everyone is able to take little steps, one after another, again and again.

It is in the little steps, repeated over and over again, that great things are accomplished.

Look at your own life and you'll see many challenges. Some may seem almost impossible to overcome. Yet, as soon as you start working on them, they begin to grow smaller. With each passing day, step by step, you begin to gain on them.

And eventually, not only has the original challenge been conquered — something even more important has happened. You have grown. You have learned. You have achieved. You have experienced. And by your own hand you have made your dreams a reality.

However great the obstacle, however ambitious the goal, there is something you can do about it today. And tomorrow, and the next day. Stop wishing for a big step, and start taking the little ones.

You'll be tired

No matter what you do today, you'll be tired when it is all over.

You can be tired after a day of effective effort and accomplishment, or you can be tired after a day of getting nowhere. The choice is yours.

If you're going to be tired anyway, it makes sense to get something out of it. To put forth your best effort, to move in the direction of your goals, to make a difference, to make a life of excellence for yourself and the world around you.

Then, along with being tired, you'll be satisfied and fulfilled, too. And you'll rest well, knowing your life is full, knowing your journey is going well.

How would you rather feel tonight — tired and frustrated, or tired and satisfied? It all depends on what you do right now, with this day that's waiting to be filled.

What are you waiting for?

Right now, today, you have everything you need to create the life you want. The only thing left to do, is to do it. Make the commitment, take the action, do whatever needs to be done to make your life count.

Anything less than the best you can be, is just cheating yourself and the world. You are special. You have something unique to offer. What is holding you back? What is keeping you from living your life to the fullest?

There will never be a better time than now, to begin to be the person you were meant to be. Make the effort. Give it your best shot. Just do it. Whatever it takes, do it. It will be difficult. It will be painful. But the pain of effort, of discipline, is minuscule compared to the pain of regret.

The time you spend today, you will never have again. You rarely regret the things you did — most regret is for the things you didn't do. Put one foot in front of the other, today, tomorrow, and the next day. Take the first step, and then the next, and don't stop until you're where you want to be.

The Daily Motivator To Go